CW00924940

A RECORD A DAY

SPORT

GUINNESS WORLD RECORDS LIMITED,
THE JIM PATTISON GROUP

Registered address:
Ground Floor, The Rookery,
2 Dyott Street, London, WC1A 1DE

First published in Great Britain in 2025 by Guinness World Records Limited

001

A catalogue record for this book is available from the British Library

ISBN 978-1-913484-87-3 (hardback)

Editor: Tom Beckerlegge

For Guinness World Records: Jane Boatfield, Chris Bryans, Craig Glenday, Matt White

Cover design: Matt Drew

Images © Shutterstock

Printed and bound in Great Britain by Clays Ltd, Elcograf S.p.A.

Introduction

Welcome to *GWR 365*, a new series of books from Guinness World Records offering a record set on every day of the calendar year. We begin by tackling sport – and where better to kick-off? So many of its major events are synonymous with a certain time of the year. Think of the Masters golf tournament at Augusta, in the first week of April. Or Wimbledon, at the height of the British summertime – sunshine, strawberries and cream... and the occasional rain delay. Baseball's "Fall Classic", aka the World Series. The Boxing Day Test Match in Australia.

But *GWR 365* isn't just a tour of the annual sporting calendar; it's a history of sport itself. From the first staging of yachting's America's Cup in 1851 – which Queen Victoria travelled to the Isle of Wight to watch – we stop by some of the great sporting milestones: the first modern Olympic Games; Don Bradman's famous duck; the Rumble in the Jungle. We've also made room for the lighter side of competition, dipping into classic GWR categories such as pogo-stick jumping, bog-snorkelling – even the Wife-Carrying World Championship! Whatever sport you love, you'll find something here for you.

Throughout *GWR 365: Sport*, you'll find tables, quotes and pull-out facts digging deeper behind the records. We've also shone a light on some of sport's unsung characters: the astronaut who ran a marathon in space; the sumo wrestler who suffered an embarrassing wardrobe malfunction; the cyclist who won a race while on the run from a WWII prison camp. Their stories remind us that sport doesn't happen in a bubble – it's part of the wider fabric of our lives.

But enough of the pre-match pleasantries – the teams are in the tunnel and waiting to get out on to the pitch. Time to get the action underway...

Tom Beckerlegge,
Sports Editor, Guinness World Records

1 JANUARY

Staged outdoors at Michigan Stadium in Ann Arbor, USA, the 2014 Winter Classic drew the **highest attendance for an NHL game** – 104,173 people. The huge crowd watched the Toronto Maple Leafs (CAN) defeat the Detroit Red Wings (USA) 3–2 after a shootout, with Canadian centre Tyler Bozak scoring the game-winner.

As of 1 Mar 2025, a total of 43 outdoor matches had been staged by the NHL since 2003. The New York Rangers boasted the best record, winning all five games they had played to date.

2 JANUARY

During a 1932 rugby union Test match between England and South Africa at Twickenham, Springbok full-back Gerry Brand kicked the **longest drop goal** from a distance of 77.7 m (254 ft 11 in). The monster strike – at that time worth four points – helped South Africa to a 7–0 victory.

3 JANUARY

In 1972, tennis star Ken Rosewall (AUS, b. 2 Nov 1934) became the **oldest winner of the Australian Open men's singles**, lifting the Norman Brookes Challenge Cup aged 37 years 62 days. He had won the same event almost two decades earlier, aged 18 – making him also the **youngest winner of the Australian Open men's singles**.

Youngest Grand Slam singles champions

EVENT	PLAYER	AGE	YEAR
Australian Open	Martina Hingis (CHE, b. SVK, 30 Sep 1980)	16 years 117 days	1997
	Ken Rosewall (AUS, b. 2 Nov 1934)	18 years 76 days	1953
French Open	Monica Seles (USA, b. YUG, 2 Dec 1973)	16 years 189 days	1990
	Michael Chang (USA, b. 22 Feb 1972)	17 years 109 days	1989
Wimbledon	Charlotte "Lottie" Dod (UK, b. 24 Sep 1871)	15 years 285 days	1887
	Boris Becker (DEU, b. 22 Nov 1967)	17 years 227 days	1985
US Open	Tracy Austin (USA, b. 12 Dec 1962)	16 years 271 days	1979
	Pete Sampras (USA, b. 12 Aug 1971)	19 years 28 days	1990

4 JANUARY

Aged just 12 years 141 days, diver Fu Mingxia (CHN, b. 16 Aug 1978) claimed the women's 10 m platform title at the 1991 World Aquatics Championships in Perth, Western Australia. The rules were subsequently changed to bar under-14s from all world championship and Olympic events – meaning that her record for the **youngest diving world champion** will likely never be beaten.

5 JANUARY

In 2007, Shane Warne (AUS) brought the curtain down on his Test cricket career as Australia sealed a 5–0 Ashes whitewash over England at the Sydney Cricket Ground. The legendary leg spinner took 708 wickets in 145 Tests, then a record for any bowler. This total included 195 English wickets – which remains the **most wickets taken by a bowler against one team in Test cricket**.

Warne's wickets

OPPONENT	MATCHES	WICKETS	OPPONENT	MATCHES	WICKETS
England	36	195	Sri Lanka	13	59
South Africa	24	130	India	14	43
New Zealand	20	103	Bangladesh	2	11
Pakistan	15	90	Zimbabwe	1	6
West Indies	19	65	ICC World XI	1	6

6 JANUARY

The Indianapolis Olympians and Rochester Royals (both USA) played out the **longest NBA game** in 1951, battling through six periods of overtime for a total game time of 78 min. The Olympians eventually triumphed 75–73 at Edgerton Park Arena in Rochester, New York. Just 18 points were scored in half an hour of OT.

> In order to combat the low-action, low-scoring games that blighted the NBA in the early 1950s, a 24-sec shot clock was proposed by Danny Biasone, owner of the Syracuse Nationals. The rule, adopted on 22 Apr 1954, forced teams to shoot more often, speeding up the play and revolutionizing the game.

7 JANUARY

In his final round at the 2024 Sentry Tournament of Champions in Hawaii, Im Sung-jae (KOR) sank 11 birdies to take his tournament total to 34 – the **most birdies in a PGA Tour event**. He finished on -25, tied for fifth. One of the most scenic courses in golf, The Plantation Course at Kapalua plays a monster 7,596 yards and is the only par 73 on the PGA Tour. Low scores and big drives are commonplace.

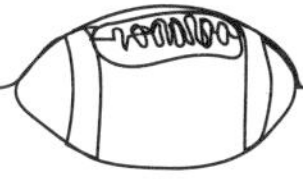

8 JANUARY

The AFC wildcard game between the 2011 Denver Broncos and Pittsburgh Steelers (both USA) was settled after just 11 sec of overtime, Denver quarterback Tim Tebow hitting Demaryius Thomas for an 80-yard touchdown to seal a 29–23 victory. This is the **shortest overtime NFL game**.

9 JANUARY

In 2016, Kurt Searvogel (USA) completed the **greatest annual distance by a male cyclist**, having covered 76,076 mi (122,432 km) – around 28 times the distance from New York City to Los Angeles. The software engineer, nicknamed "Tarzan", went through seven bikes and battled illness, five crashes and countless flat tyres to ride every day. He even logged 175 mi (281 km) on his wedding day.

The annual mileage record developed from a competition devised by *Cycling* magazine in 1911. The record was held for 77 years by Englishman Tommy Godwin, a former grocer's delivery boy who cycled 120,805 km (75,065 mi) in 1939.

10 JANUARY

In 2020, Claressa Shields (USA) defeated Ivana Habazin to win the vacant WBC and WBO women's super-welterweight titles in her 10th pro bout. Shields had previously won belts at super-middleweight and middleweight – meaning that she also claimed the record for the **fewest fights to become a three-weight boxing world champion**.

11 JANUARY

At the 1982 Lada Classic in Oldham, UK, Steve Davis (UK) compiled the **first snooker 147 break in professional competition**. During his quarter-final match against John Spencer, "The Nugget" potted 15 reds with 15 blacks and cleared up the colours to score the maximum possible points in a break. He won a Lada car for his efforts.

"I bet Steve can see... the pocket closing up and closing up and getting smaller."

(Commentator John Pulman, on the final black of Davis's historic 147 break)

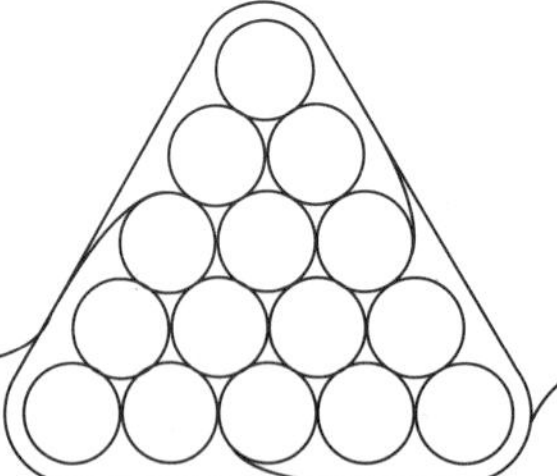

12 JANUARY

In 2020, Manchester City marksman Sergio Agüero (ARG) claimed the outright record for the **most English Premier League hat-tricks**, bagging three goals for the 12th time during City's 6–1 win over Aston Villa. Previously, Agüero had been tied with Alan Shearer, who hit 11 hat-tricks between 1993 and 1999 while playing for Blackburn Rovers and Newcastle United.

Agüero at the treble

OPPONENT	DATE	FINAL SCORE
Wigan Athletic	10 Sep 2011	3–0
Tottenham Hotspur	18 Oct 2014	4–1
Queens Park Rangers	10 May 2015	6–0
Newcastle United	3 Oct 2015	6–1
Chelsea	16 Apr 2016	3–0
Watford	16 Sep 2017	6–0
Newcastle United	20 Jan 2018	3–1
Leicester City	10 Feb 2018	5–1
Huddersfield Town	19 Aug 2018	6–1
Arsenal	3 Feb 2019	3–1
Chelsea	10 Feb 2019	6–0
Aston Villa	12 Jan 2020	6–1

13 JANUARY

At Super Bowl VIII in 1974, the Miami Dolphins (USA) used their ground game to outmuscle the Minnesota Vikings 24–7 at Houston's Rice Stadium. Having scored rushing touchdowns on their first two drives, the Dolphins proceeded to make the **fewest passing attempts by a team in a Super Bowl game** – seven. Dolphins quarterback Bob Griese finished with six out of seven completions, for 73 yards. He threw just one pass in the entire second half.

> *"I knew we were in trouble after their first drive."*
>
> (Minnesota coach Bud Grant, after losing Super Bowl VIII to the Miami Dolphins)

14 JANUARY

During the Detroit Red Wings' 3–0 victory over the Toronto Maple Leafs in 1945, Harry Lumley (CAN, b. 11 Nov 1926) became the **youngest NHL goaltender to record a shutout**, aged 18 years 64 days. Lumley, a future Vezina Trophy winner, was nicknamed "Apple Cheeks" on account of his rosy complexion – not helped by his tendency to lose his temper after conceding a goal.

15 JANUARY

Stéphane Peterhansel (FRA) extended his record for the **most Dakar Rally wins** to 14 in 2021, securing his eighth victory in the car class. He has also triumphed in the motorcycle category on six occasions. Uniquely, Peterhansel has won the iconic rally on three different continents: Africa, South America and Asia.

The Dakar Rally was the brainchild of Thierry Sabine, who was inspired after spending three days lost in the Ténéré desert during the 1977 Rallye Côte-Côte. The first Rallye Paris-Dakar was held two years later.

16 JANUARY

At 2021's UFC Fight Island 7 in Abu Dhabi, UAE, Max Holloway (USA) unleashed the **most significant strikes landed during a UFC match** – 445. He attempted 744 blows in a five-round blizzard of violence against Calvin Kattar, landing 141 strikes in Round 4 alone. Holloway, nicknamed "Blessed", duly won the featherweight bout by unanimous decision.

UFC's top single-bout strikers

FIGHTER	OPPONENT	EVENT	SIG. STRIKES
Max Holloway	Calvin Kattar	UFC Fight Island 7	445
Max Holloway	Brian Ortega	UFC 231	290
Rob Font	Marlon Vera	UFC on ESPN 35	271
Jared Cannonier	Marvin Vettori	UFC on ESPN 47	241
Nate Diaz	Donald Cerrone	UFC 141	238

17 JANUARY

In 1937, US golfer Patty Berg won the inaugural Titleholders Championship to secure her first major tournament victory. She finished three shots clear of Dorothy Kirby at Augusta Country Club in Georgia, USA. Berg would go on to achieve the **most women's major golf titles** – 15, including six further wins at the Titleholders Championship.

18 JANUARY

Max Günther (DEU, b. 2 Jul 1997) took the chequered flag at the 2020 Santiago ePrix in Chile to become the **youngest driver to win a Formula E race**, aged 22 years 200 days. In a dramatic finish, Günther retook the lead from António Félix da Costa on the final lap to claim a historic victory.

19 JANUARY

In 2013, skier Johan Clarey (FRA) was clocked at 161.9 km/h (100.6 mph) on the Lauberhorn course at the Wengen downhill in Switzerland. This is the **fastest speed at the FIS Alpine Ski World Cup**. Clarey became the first skier to break the 100-mph barrier.

> At the Beijing Winter Olympics in 2022, Johan Clarey (b. 8 Jan 1981) became the **oldest Olympic medallist in Alpine skiing**. He claimed a silver in the men's downhill aged 41 years 30 days. It was Clarey's fourth Olympic Games; his previous best finish had been 18th.

20 JANUARY

Kristýna Plíšková (CZE) served the **most aces in a Women's Tennis Association match** – 31 – during her second-round encounter against Monica Puig at the Australian Open in 2016. But Plíšková's high-speed barrage was in vain, as she squandered five match points and lost 6–4, 6–7, 7–9. Three years later, she managed to fire off 28 aces to record the second-highest total in a WTA match, only to lose again – once more to Monica Puig.

21 JANUARY

At the 2018 CareerBuilder Challenge in California, USA, Mark Brooks (USA) made his 803rd and final appearance on the PGA Tour – the **most starts** in the organization's history. Brooks, who joined the tour in 1983, won seven events including one major – the 1996 PGA Championship, following a sudden-death play-off with Kenny Perry.

22 JANUARY

In 2023, Laura Enever (AUS) achieved the **largest wave surfed paddle-in by a woman**, riding a 13.3-m-high (43-ft 7-in) breaker on the Hawaiian island of Oahu's North Shore. While waiting as an alternate competitor at the Eddie Aikau Big Wave Invitational, Enever decided to paddle to the outer reefs, only to catch a record-breaking swell. Her feat was confirmed by the World Surf League.

> *"I knew it was the wave of my life, the way it all came together and the way I committed, backed myself, told myself to go..."*
>
> (Laura Enever)

23 JANUARY

In 1958, Pakistan opener Hanif Mohammad completed the **longest men's Test cricket innings**, batting for 16 hr 10 min against the West Indies in Bridgetown, Barbados. Following on 473 runs behind, Mohammad's marathon knock of 337 helped Pakistan to a second innings total of 657 for 8 declared; the match was drawn.

24 JANUARY

Adrenaline junkie Chase Boehringer (USA) achieved the **fastest speed volcano surfing** in 2021. Riding a stainless-steel-bottomed sandboard, he hit 45.06 km/h (27.99 mph) on the ash-covered slopes of Parícutin, a cinder-cone volcano in the Mexican state of Michoacán.

25 JANUARY

At Super Bowl XV in 1981, the Oakland Raiders defeated the Philadelphia Eagles 27–10 at the Louisiana Superdome in New Orleans. Raiders linebacker Rod Martin (USA) picked off quarterback Ron "Jaws" Jaworski three times, including his first pass of the game. This remains the **most interceptions in a Super Bowl**.

26 JANUARY

In 1924, Charles Jewtraw (USA) became the **first Winter Olympic gold medallist**, winning the 500 m speed skating at the inaugural Games in Chamonix, France. Although a two-time US champion, the 23-year-old Jewtraw had actually retired from skating and had never raced over 500 m before. Yet the underdog sprinted to victory – and Olympic immortality – in a time of exactly 44 sec.

1924 Winter Olympic champions

SPORT	EVENT	GOLD MEDALLIST(S)
Bobsleigh	Men's team	Switzerland
Curling	Men's team	Great Britain
Ice hockey	Men's team	Canada
Figure skating	Men's singles	Gillis Grafström (SWE)
	Women's singles	Herma Szabo-Plank (AUT)
	Pairs skating	Helene Engelmann and Alfred Berger (both AUT)
Speed skating	500 m	Charles Jewtraw (USA)
	1,500 m	Clas Thunberg (FIN)
	5,000 m	Clas Thunberg
	10,000 m	Julius Skutnabb (FIN)
	All-round	Clas Thunberg
Nordic skiing	Military patrol	Switzerland
	Cross-country skiing (18 km)	Thorleif Haug (NOR)
	Cross-country skiing (50 km)	Thorleif Haug
	Nordic combined	Thorleif Haug
	Ski jumping	Jacob Tullin Thams (NOR)

27 JANUARY

Carl Lewis (USA) recorded the **farthest men's indoor long jump** – 8.79 m (28 ft 10 in) – at the 1984 Millrose Games in New York City. Battling a cold and struggling with his rhythm on the wooden runway, Lewis had been in second place with one jump remaining. But in the final round he pulled out one of the all-time great long jumps, beating his own indoor world record by 23 cm. Lewis would go unbeaten in the event for a decade, winning 65 consecutive competitions.

> *"You have to be able to do it. You have to be able to come from behind. A true champion can win in any way."*
>
> (Carl Lewis)

28 JANUARY

In 1990, the San Francisco 49ers (USA) ran up the **highest Super Bowl score**, thrashing the Denver Broncos 55–10 to win Super Bowl XXIV. Wide receiver Jerry Rice became the first player to score three receiving touchdowns on Super Sunday – a record he himself would equal five years later, against the San Diego Chargers at Super Bowl XXIX.

29 JANUARY

The **first Winter Olympic women's gold medallist** was crowned in 1924 when Herma Szabo-Plank (AUT) won the ladies' figure skating in Chamonix, France. She took to the ice in a short skirt to aid her movement – a pioneering act that would later be misattributed to Szabo-Plank's rival, Sonja Henie (who finished last in Chamonix, at the age of just 11).

30 JANUARY

In 2003, wheelchair tennis player Esther Vergeer (NLD) suffered a defeat against Daniela Di Toro at the Sydney International. Vergeer would not lose another singles match again, embarking on an extraordinary 10-year winning streak and racking up the **most consecutive women's wheelchair singles match wins** – 470. She was victorious in 120 tournaments, including 21 Grand Slams and four Paralympics.

31 JANUARY

At Winter X Games XX in 2016, Lindsey Jacobellis (USA) claimed her 10th gold medal in snowboard cross in Aspen, Colorado, USA. This is the **most women's X Games gold medals in winter disciplines**. Jacobellis crossed the line just 0.41 sec ahead of Eva Samková.

1 FEBRUARY

Quarterback Peyton Manning (USA) extended his record for the **most wins of the NFL Most Valuable Player award** to five following the 2013 season. It was his first with the Denver Broncos, having earned the previous four playing for the Indianapolis Colts between 2003 (shared with Tennessee Titans QB Steve McNair, in a rare tie) and 2009.

2 FEBRUARY

In 1977, Ian "Bull" Turnbull (CAN) scored the **most goals by a defenseman in an NHL game** – five – for the Toronto Maple Leafs during their 9–1 dismantling of the Detroit Red Wings. Turnbull became the first player in league history to score five times from five shots.

3 FEBRUARY

In 2018, a United States team comprising Chrishuna Williams, Raevyn Rogers, Charlene Lipsey and Ajeé Wilson ran the **fastest women's indoor 4 x 800 m**, completing 16 laps of a 200-m track in 8 min 5.89 sec. They were competing at the prestigious Millrose Games in New York City, USA.

> *That is the loudest I've ever heard [the crowd]. That was insane. Every lap was high energy.*
>
> (Ajeé Wilson)

4 FEBRUARY

During his 12-round IBF featherweight title bout against Jorge Páez in 1990, Troy Dorsey (USA) landed the **most punches in a championship boxing match**. Dorsey connected with an astonishing 620 blows out of 1,365 thrown – averaging 52 every round – and still lost the fight. Páez won a split decision, despite landing 280 fewer punches.

5 FEBRUARY

At the 2022 Billabong Pro Pipeline in Hawaii, USA, surfing legend Kelly Slater (USA) won his 56th and final World Surf League event days before his 50th birthday. Slater defeated Seth Moniz in the final to seal his eighth Billabong title, 30 years after his first. He still holds the record for the **most World Surf League event wins**.

Kelly Slater had a recurring role in '90s TV juggernaut *Baywatch*, playing surfer Jimmy Slade. A talented guitarist, he has performed on-stage with Jack Johnson and grunge royalty Pearl Jam, and also featured in the video for Garbage's 1999 single "You Look So Fine".

6 FEBRUARY

In 2020, veteran ten-pin bowler Carmen Salvino (USA, b. 23 Nov 1933) took part in the Tournament of Champions aged 86 years 75 days. The **oldest bowler at a PBA Tour event**, he finished 59th out of 62 entrants at AMF Riviera Lanes in Fairlawn, Ohio, USA. A founder member of the Professional Bowlers Association and 17-time titlist, Salvino was competing in his 734th PBA event.

7 FEBRUARY

At Super Bowl LV in 2021, the Tampa Bay Buccaneers overcame the Kansas City Chiefs 31–9 to extend quarterback Tom Brady's (USA) record for the **most Super Bowl wins** to seven. Brady had won his previous six championship rings with the New England Patriots. He also increased his record for the **most wins of the Super Bowl MVP** to five.

Brady's Super Bowl wins

SUPER BOWL	OPPONENT	SCORE	LOCATION	SEASON
XXXVI*	St Louis Rams	20–17	New Orleans, Louisiana	2001
XXXVIII*	Carolina Panthers	32–29	Houston, Texas	2003
XXXIX	Philadelphia Eagles	24–21	Jacksonville, Florida	2004
XLIX*	Seattle Seahawks	28–24	Glendale, Arizona	2014
LI*	Atlanta Falcons	34–28	Houston, Texas	2016
LIII	Los Angeles Rams	13–3	Atlanta, Georgia	2018
LV*	Kansas City Chiefs	31–9	Tampa, Florida	2020

**Brady voted Super Bowl MVP*

8 FEBRUARY

At the age of 15 years 69 days, East German speed skater Andrea Mitscherlich (b. 1 Dec 1960) won silver in the women's 3,000 m at the 1976 Winter Olympics in Innsbruck, Austria. The **youngest Winter Olympic women's individual medallist**, Mitscherlich went on to take part in four Games, winning a total of seven medals.

> **Andrea Mitscherlich is the only Winter Olympian to win medals under three different names: she competed as Andrea Schöne in 1984 and Andrea Ehrig in 1988.**

9 FEBRUARY

Sprinter Donovan Bailey (CAN, b. JAM) blitzed the **fastest men's 50 m** in 5.56 sec at the 1996 Reno Air Games in Nevada, USA. This rarely run event is the shortest track race monitored by World Athletics. Bailey, who began training as a sprinter while working as a stockbroker, went on to win 100 m gold at the 1996 Olympics in Atlanta, in a then-world-record time of 9.84 sec.

10 FEBRUARY

At the 1970 Africa Cup of Nations, Côte d'Ivoire striker Laurent Pokou hit five goals as "The Elephants" trampled Ethiopia 6–1 in Khartoum, Sudan. Pokou finished the tournament as top scorer, with eight. His haul against Ethiopia remains the **most goals by a player in an Africa Cup of Nations game**.

11 FEBRUARY

In 2020, Maya Gabeira (BRA) rode the **largest wave surfed by a woman** – 22.4 m (73 ft 5 in) in height – during the World Surf League's Nazaré Tow Surfing Challenge in Portugal. Nazaré's Praia do Norte (North Beach) has become a magnet for surfers owing to its huge waves, which are caused by a deep undersea canyon that channels the swell as it heads for shore. Gabeira survived a brush with death there in 2013, when she was knocked unconscious after falling from a 70-ft wave and had CPR administered on the beach.

> *"The fastest I've been on a surfboard, and the noise by far the loudest, most scary thing I've ever been riding on."*
>
> (Maya Gabeira, on her record-breaking wave)

12 FEBRUARY

At Super Bowl LVII in 2023, Jason and Travis Kelce (both USA) became the **first brothers to play against one another at a Super Bowl**, lining up for the Philadelphia Eagles and the Kansas City Chiefs respectively. It was Travis who took the family honours, with the Chiefs prevailing 38–35 at State Farm Stadium in Glendale, Arizona. The siblings' mother, Donna – aka "Mama Kelce" – watched on wearing a jacket sporting both team colours.

13 FEBRUARY

At the 2018 Winter Olympics in Pyeongchang, South Korea, snowboarder Chloe Kim (USA) announced herself to the sporting world. During the women's halfpipe competition at Bogwang Phoenix Park, she landed back-to-back 1080s on her final run to earn a score of 98.25 – 8.5 points ahead of the rest of the field. Kim (b. 23 Apr 2000) was aged 17 years 296 days, making her the **youngest women's snowboarding gold medallist at a Winter Olympics.**

14 FEBRUARY

In 2005, Arsenal strolled to a 5–1 league win over Crystal Palace, having selected the **first all-foreign English Premier League squad**. A total of eight countries were represented in the 16-man unit, led by six Frenchmen and three Spaniards. Much had changed since the EPL's first weekend, on 15–16 Aug 1992, when only 13 players from outside the British Isles were involved across the league.

Class of '92: the EPL's first foreign players

TEAM	PLAYER	NATIONALITY
Arsenal	John Jensen	Denmark
	Anders Limpar	Sweden
Everton	Robert Warzycha	Poland
Ipswich Town	Craig Forrest	Canada
Leeds United	Eric Cantona	France
Liverpool	Ronnie Rosenthal	Israel
Manchester City	Michel Vonk	Netherlands
Manchester United	Andrei Kanchelskis	Russia
	Peter Schmeichel	Denmark
Oldham Athletic	Gunnar Halle	Norway
Queens Park Rangers	Jan Stejskal	Czechoslovakia
Sheffield Wednesday	Roland Nilsson	Sweden
Wimbledon	Hans Segers	Netherlands

15 FEBRUARY

Leon Spinks (USA) became world heavyweight boxing champion in 1978 after outpointing title holder Muhammad Ali at the Las Vegas Hilton. It was only Spinks's eighth professional bout – the **fewest fights to win the men's world heavyweight boxing championship**. The reigning Olympic champion at light heavyweight, Spinks had fought his first pro contest just 396 days earlier.

16 FEBRUARY

At the 1992 Games in Albertville, France, ski jumper Toni Nieminen (FIN, b. 31 May 1975) became the **youngest men's individual gold medallist at the Winter Olympics**. He won the men's individual large hill competition aged 16 years 261 days old. It was actually Nieminen's second gold of the Games, having been part of Finland's victorious large hill team two days beforehand.

Nieminen's golden performances at the Winter Olympics catapulted him to stardom back home in Finland. Upon his triumphant return, he needed a police escort to protect him from teenage fans. He was granted special government dispensation to drive a car to training, even though he hadn't reached 18 – the legal age for driving in Finland.

17 FEBRUARY

Fly-half Jonny Wilkinson (UK) racked up the **most points in a men's Six Nations rugby match** – 35 – as England trounced Italy 80–23 at Twickenham in 2001. Wilkinson kicked four penalties and nine conversions and also went over for a try. He went on to score a tournament-record 89 points in five games as England won the championship. They were denied the Grand Slam by Ireland, however, in a match postponed to October on account of an outbreak of foot-and-mouth disease.

Jonny Wilkinson at the 2001 Six Nations

OPPONENT	SCORE	PENS	CONS	TRIES	POINTS
Wales	44–15	2	4		14
Italy	80–23	4	9	1	35
Scotland	43–3	1	5		13
France	48–19	2	6		18
Ireland	14–20	3			9

18 FEBRUARY

In 2021, Nouria Newman (FRA) braved the **highest women's waterfall descent by kayak**, plunging 31.69 m (104 ft) down Don Wilo's Falls on the Río Pucuno in Ecuador. Newman, a former gold medallist at the 2014 ICF Canoe Slalom World Championships, is the first woman to run a 100-ft waterfall. Her history-making descent earned her a fifth consecutive Rider of Year title at the Whitewater Awards.

19 FEBRUARY

At the 2002 Games in Salt Lake City, Utah, USA, Vonetta Flowers (USA) became the **first Black gold medallist at the Winter Olympics**, teaming up with Jill Bakken to win the two-woman bobsleigh event. Formally a sprinter and long jumper who had qualified for the US Summer Olympic trials, Flowers first attended a bobsleigh try-out in 2000 – just two months later, she was competing internationally.

"It felt like I had been placed in a trash can and thrown down a hill. I was scared out of my mind."

(Vonetta Flowers, on her first time in a bobsleigh)

20 FEBRUARY

Playing against Australia in 2016, New Zealand captain Brendon McCullum smashed the **fastest men's Test match hundred** in just 54 balls at Hagley Oval in Christchurch, New Zealand. McCullum's 79-min century, which came in his 101st and final Test, contained four sixes and 16 fours.

In a Test match against South Africa in 1999, New Zealand tail-ender Geoff Allott faced 77 balls without scoring a single run. His 101-min-long duck took 23 deliveries more than Brendon McCullum needed to compile his record-breaking century against Australia.

21 FEBRUARY

The **closest finish to the Daytona 500** occurred in 2016, when Denny Hamlin took the chequered flag ahead of Martin Truex Jr (both USA) by just 0.010 sec after 500 mi (805 km) of racing. It was the 58th running of "The Great American Race", staged at Daytona International Speedway in Florida, USA. The most prestigious event in US stock-car racing, the Daytona 500 was first held in 1959 and acts as the traditional curtain-raiser to the NASCAR season.

22 FEBRUARY

At the 2003 Cricket World Cup, Pakistani pace bowler Shoaib Akhtar – aka the "Rawalpindi Express" – unleashed the **fastest cricket delivery** in history in Cape Town, South Africa. The final ball of his second over, a maiden to England's Nick Knight, was clocked on a speed gun at a blistering 161.3 km/h (100.2 mph). The slowest of Shoaib's six deliveries was timed at 153.3 km/h (95.2 mph).

> *"The method to bowling quick is to enjoy it. The roar of the crowd always used to drive me nuts."*
>
> (Shoaib Akhtar)

23 FEBRUARY

At the 1980 Winter Olympics in the US resort of Lake Placid, Eric Heiden (USA) completed a remarkable sweep of the men's speed skating events, adding the 10,000 m to his titles at 500 m, 1,000 m, 1,500 m and 5,000 m. This is the **most gold medals at a single Winter Olympics**. Heiden set Olympic records in every event and destroyed the 10,000 m world record by 6.2 sec.

> **After retiring from speed skating, Eric Heiden took up road and track cycling. He won the first US Professional Cycling Championship in 1985 and competed in the 1986 Tour de France, crashing out during a descent in the Alps in the latter stages of the race.**

24 FEBRUARY

In 2018, a 2–1 defeat for West Bromwich Albion against Huddersfield Town signalled Gareth Barry's (UK) 653rd and final game in top-flight football – the **most appearances in the English Premier League**. Barry had made his league debut almost 20 years earlier, on 2 May 1998, for Aston Villa. He also played for Manchester City and Everton, racking up more than 50,000 min of game time.

25 FEBRUARY

Cross-country skier Marit Bjørgen (NOR) increased her record for the **most Winter Olympic medals** to 15 in the final event of the 2018 Games – the women's 30 km mass start – in Pyeongchang, South Korea. Bjørgen medalled at five consecutive Olympics between 2002 and 2018, amassing eight golds, four silvers and three bronze.

Winter Olympic medal leaders

ATHLETE	SPORT	MEDALS	OLYMPICS
Marit Bjørgen (NOR)	Cross-country skiing	15 (8G, 4S, 3B)	2002–18
Ole Einar Bjørndalen (NOR)	Biathlon	13 (8G, 4S, 1B)	1994–2014
Ireen Wüst (NLD)	Speed skating	13 (6G, 5S, 2B)	2006–22
Bjørn Dæhlie (NOR)	Cross-country skiing	12 (8G, 4S)	1988–98
Arianna Fontana (ITA)	Short track speed skating	11 (2G, 4S, 5B)	2006–22

26 FEBRUARY

During the 1887 Home Nations Championship in rugby, Scotland's George Lindsay scored five tries in one match against Wales. Lindsay, a back noted for his pace and kicking out of hand, was a former captain of Oxford University. Nearly 140 years later - and two changes of tournament name – Lindsay still holds the record for the **most tries by a player in a Six Nations Championship game**.

27 FEBRUARY

LeBron James (USA, b. 30 Dec 1984) claimed the record for the **youngest NBA player to score 10,000 points** in 2008. He scored 26 points for the Cleveland Cavaliers against the Boston Celtics to reach the milestone at the age of 23 years 59 days, breaking the previous record of Kobe Bryant by more than a year. "King James" has been the youngest player to reach every 1,000-point milestone in NBA history.

28 FEBRUARY

At UFC 184 in 2015, Ronda Rousey (USA) completed the **fastest UFC title-fight victory by submission**. She locked in an armbar to defeat Cat Zingano after just 14 sec of their bantamweight clash at the Staples Center in Los Angeles, California, USA. Rousey, an Olympic judo bronze medallist, was the first female fighter signed by the UFC. She defended her bantamweight title six times before losing to Holly Holm in a shock upset at UFC 193.

Rousey's brutal bantamweight defences

OPPONENT	EVENT	ROUND	METHOD
Liz Carmouche	UFC 157	1	Submission
Miesha Tate	UFC 168	3	Submission
Sara McMann	UFC 170	1	TKO
Alexis Davis	UFC 175	1	KO
Cat Zingano	UFC 184	1	Submission
Bethe Correia	UFC 190	1	KO

29 FEBRUARY

On Leap Day in 2020, Julio Cesar Martínez and Jay Harris fought for the WBC flyweight title in Frisco, Texas, USA. At ringside was the **oldest judge in a world championship boxing fight** – Herb Santos (USA, b. 15 Aug 1931), who was 88 years 198 days old. He and the other two judges awarded Martínez the bout by unanimous decision.

1 MARCH

Garfield Sobers (BRB) compiled his first Test century in style in 1958, scoring 365 not out against Pakistan at Sabina Park in Kingston, Jamaica. The 21-year-old all-rounder hit 38 fours, pushing the West Indies to a total of 790 for 3 declared. Sobers' astonishing knock broke Len Hutton's record for the highest individual innings by one run, and remains the **highest men's maiden Test cricket century**.

Men's Test innings record progression

SCORE	PLAYER	MATCH	YEAR
165*	Charles Bannerman	AUSTRALIA vs England	1877
211	Billy Murdoch	England vs AUSTRALIA	1884
287	RE Foster	Australia vs ENGLAND	1903
325	Andy Sandham	West Indies vs ENGLAND	1930
334	Don Bradman	England vs AUSTRALIA	1930
336*	Wally Hammond	New Zealand vs ENGLAND	1933
364	Len Hutton	ENGLAND vs Australia	1938
365*	Garfield Sobers	WEST INDIES vs Pakistan	1958
375	Brian Lara	WEST INDIES vs England	1994
380	Matthew Hayden	AUSTRALIA vs Zimbabwe	2003
400*	Brian Lara	WEST INDIES vs England	2004

2 MARCH

In 1962, Wilt Chamberlain (USA) scored the **most points in an NBA game** – 100 – during the Philadelphia Warriors' 169–147 victory over the New York Knicks at Hershey Sports Arena in Pennsylvania, USA. The 7-ft 1-in-tall (2.16-m) centre reached his century with 46 sec left on the fourth-quarter clock. He broke his own single-game record of 78 points, set three months earlier.

3 MARCH

The Montreal Canadiens demolished the Quebec Bulldogs 16–3 in 1920 to record the **most goals in an NHL game**. Four Canadiens – Didier Pitre, Odie Cleghorn, Newsy Lalonde and Harry Cameron – helped themselves to a hat-trick. "Quebec Defeated in Uninteresting Game", declared the *Montreal Gazette* the following day.

4 MARCH

In 2004, a field of 11 intrepid runners descended 212 m (695 ft) into the Bochnia salt mine in Poland to take part in the **deepest half-marathon**. The subterranean sprinters completed around eight-and-a-half laps of a 2.4-km-long (1.5-mi) track running through the mine, which is also a UNESCO World Heritage Site.

5 MARCH

In 1877, Wales played their first home international football match – a 2–0 defeat to Scotland – at the Racecourse Ground (Cae Ras in Welsh) in Wrexham. The stadium still plays host to the national side today, almost 150 years later, making it the **oldest international football ground**.

6 MARCH

The **youngest boxing world champion** was crowned in 1976. Wilfred Benítez (PRI, b. USA, 12 Sep 1958) defeated Antonio Cervantes in San Juan, Puerto Rico, to take the WBA light welterweight belt at the age of 17 years 176 days. Cervantes had made 10 consecutive defences of his title and was the heavy pre-fight favourite. However, it was Benítez who won the bout on a split decision after 15 rounds of seesawing action, having displayed the defensive prowess that earned him the nickname "El Radar".

Wilfred Benítez would go on to become a three-weight world champion by the age of just 22, winning the WBC welterweight and super welterweight titles.

7 MARCH

Roy Makaay (NLD) scored the **fastest UEFA Champions League goal** in 2007, striking after just 10.12 sec of Bayern Munich's Round of 16 second-leg tie against Real Madrid in Munich. The home side prevailed 2–1 and progressed to the quarter-finals on away goals.

Lightning strikes in the Champions League

PLAYER	MATCH	DATE	TIME
Roy Makaay	BAYERN MUNICH vs Real Madrid	7 Mar 2007	10.12 sec
Jonas	VALENCIA vs Bayer Leverkusen	1 Nov 2011	10.96 sec
Gilberto Silva	PSV Eindhoven vs ARSENAL	25 Sep 2002	20.07 sec
Alessandro Del Piero	Manchester United vs JUVENTUS	1 Oct 1997	20.12 sec
Clarence Seedorf	FC Schalke 04 vs AC MILAN	28 Sep 2005	21.06 sec

8 MARCH

In 1997, rugby union player Gavin Lawless (ZAF) enjoyed one of the great sporting debuts. Taking to the field for Natal Sharks's Super 12 clash against Otago Highlanders in Durban, the full-back went over for four tries and kicked nine conversions and four penalties to record the **most individual points in a Super Rugby match** – 50. The Sharks devoured the Highlanders 75–43.

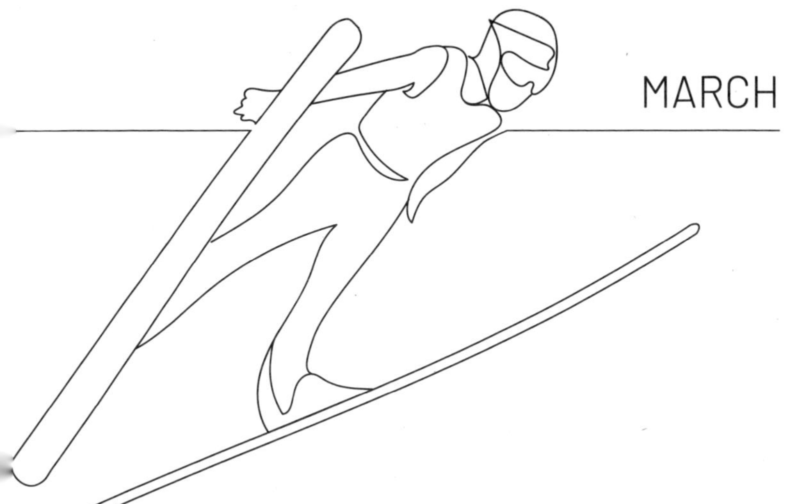

9 MARCH

In 1980, Steve Collins (CAN, b. 13 Mar 1964) became the **youngest winner of an FIS Ski Jumping World Cup men's event**. He triumphed in the men's large hill competition in Lahti, Finland, at the age of 15 years 362 days. In 10 seasons of competition, Collins never won another World Cup event.

10 MARCH

Eva Clarke (AUS) executed the **most pull-ups by a woman in an hour** in 2016, performing 725 at Al Wahda Mall in Abu Dhabi, UAE. The fitness instructor and multiple GWR title holder went on to complete a bicep-busting 3,737 pull-ups over the course of 24 hr – a then-record.

11 MARCH

During a bruising encounter between the Los Angeles Kings and the Philadelphia Flyers in 1979, Kings enforcer Randy Holt (CAN) racked up the **most penalty minutes in an NHL game** – 67 – all in a single period. The combustible defenseman was involved in a series of brawls with the so-called "Broad Street Bullies", incurring a total of nine penalties. Holt was ejected from the game following the end of the first period.

Randy Holt vs the Broad Street Bullies

TIME	OFFENCE	PENALTY
10:25	Holding	2 min
14:58	Fighting (vs Bathe)	5 min
14:58	Misconduct	10 min
19:58	Fighting (vs Bathe)	5 min
20:00	Fighting (vs Holmgren)	5 min
20:00	Misconduct	10 min
20:00	Game misconduct	10 min
20:00	Game misconduct	10 min
20:00	Game misconduct	10 min

12 MARCH

Yohann Diniz (FRA) completed the **fastest 50,000 m men's race walk** in 2011, clocking a time of 3 hr 35 min 27.20 sec at the Georges Hébert stadium in the French city of Reims. Diniz covered 125 laps of the track, breaking the previous record of his compatriot Thierry Toutain by more than five minutes.

13 MARCH

In 1963, a 21-year-old Muhammad Ali (USA) – then fighting as Cassius Clay – outpointed Doug Jones in their heavyweight boxing clash at Madison Square Garden in New York City. The bout was voted 1963's "Fight of the Year" by *The Ring* magazine, the first of six such fights that Ali would go on to contest. This is the **most participations in *The Ring's* "Fight of the Year"**.

Ali's Fights of the Year

YEAR	OPPONENT	RESULT	ROUND
1963	Doug Jones	Win (decision)	10
1964	Sonny Liston	Win (retired)	6
1971	Joe Frazier	Loss (decision)	15
1974*	George Foreman	Win (KO)	8
1975**	Joe Frazier	Win (retired)	14
1978	Leon Spinks	Loss (decision)	15

**aka "The Rumble in the Jungle"*

***aka the "Thrilla in Manila"*

14 MARCH

The 1974 Africa Cup of Nations was won by Zaire (now the Democratic Republic of the Congo), who defeated Zambia 2–0 in a final replay in Cairo, Egypt. Both goals were scored by forward Ndaye Mulamba, who registered his eighth and ninth strikes of the tournament. This is the **most goals by a player in a single Africa Cup of Nations**.

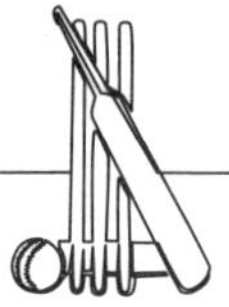

15 MARCH

In 1877, an English touring party of cricketers led by James Lillywhite took on a Grand Combined Melbourne and Sydney XI at the Melbourne Cricket Ground. This is recognized as the **first Test cricket match**. Australia won the match by 45 runs, with Charles Bannerman scoring the format's first century. More than 2,500 Tests have since been played.

As cricket's first-ever Test got underway, James Lillywhite's first-choice wicketkeeper, Edward "Ted" Pooley, was languishing in a New Zealand prison cell. Pooley had been arrested following a dispute over a wager he had struck during a warm-up match in Christchurch – which Pooley himself had ended up umpiring.

16 MARCH

At the 2001 Standard Register Ping tournament, Annika Sörenstam (SWE) shot the **lowest round at an LPGA Tour event**, completing 18 holes in just 59 strokes – the first sub-60 round in the history of women's golf. Starting on the back nine, Sörenstam kicked off with eight consecutive birdies and made 13 overall at Moon Valley Country Club in Phoenix, Arizona, USA.

Sorenstam's sensational scorecard

HOLE	**1**	**2**	**3**	**4**	**5**	**6**	**7**	**8**	**9**	**FRONT**
SHOTS	③	②	③	④	3	4	④	4	4	31
SCORE	-9	-10	-11	-12	-12	-12	-12	-13	-13	-5

HOLE	**10**	**11**	**12**	**13**	**14**	**15**	**16**	**17**	**18**	**BACK**
SHOTS	④	②	③	④	③	②	③	③	4	28
SCORE	-1	-2	-3	-4	-5	-6	-7	-8	-8	-8

17 MARCH

In 1897, Victorian pugilist Bob Fitzsimmons (UK) laid out James J Corbett with a body punch in the 14th round of their title fight in Carson City, Nevada, USA. Weighing just 167 lb (75 kg), "Ruby Robert" was the **lightest heavyweight boxing world champion** in history.

> All 14 rounds were caught on a 100-min documentary, *The Corbett–Fitzsimmons Fight* (USA, 1897), which was the longest film ever shot at that time. It was a smash hit, generating more money than the fight's gate receipts. Only fragments of the film survive today.

18 MARCH

At the 2023 Six Nations Championship, Wales captain Alun Wyn Jones played his 170th and final international game – a 41–28 defeat against France. This is the **most men's international rugby union appearances**. The doughty lock had made his debut 17 years earlier, against Argentina on 11 Jun 2006. He played 158 times for Wales and earned 12 caps for the British & Irish Lions.

19 MARCH

Jon "Bones" Jones (USA, b. 19 Jul 1987) became the **youngest UFC champion** in 2011, claiming the light-heavyweight title at UFC 128 aged 23 years 243 days. A late replacement for Rashad Evans, Jones dominated champion Maurício "Shogun" Rua, winning the bout via a third-round TKO.

20 MARCH

In 2010, freestyle footballer Yee Ming Low (MYS) ran the **fastest mile balancing a football on the head** in 8 min 35 sec, at MPSJ Athletics Stadium in Selangor, Malaysia. Although GWR record guidelines stated that he could lose control of the ball and restart from the same place, Yee Ming completed the distance without once letting the ball drop.

21 MARCH

In 2021, Kylian Mbappé (FRA, b. 20 Dec 1998) became the **youngest player to score 100 goals in the top division of French football**, aged 22 years 91 days. The Paris Saint-Germain hotshot claimed the record with a brace against Lyon. He had begun his Ligue 1 career with Monaco, hitting 16 league goals before moving to PSG in 2017.

22 MARCH

In 2024, Jasmin Paris (UK) became the **first female finisher of the Barkley Marathons**, navigating five 20-mi (32-km) loops of the notorious US ultramarathon in the mountains of Frozen Head State Park, Tennessee. Paris crossed the line just 99 sec before the 60-hr cut-off point. She became only the 20th runner in the history of the event to complete the full 100-mi (161-km) distance.

> The Barkley Marathons is the brainchild of Gary "Lazarus Lake" Cantrell, who was inspired by the 1977 prison break by James Earl Ray, the man convicted of killing Martin Luther King Jr. Ray went on the run in the Tennessee mountains for 54 hr, covering around 8 mi (12.8 km) before his recapture.

23 MARCH

During a game between the Chicago Blackhawks and the New York Rangers in 1952, Chicago's Bill Mosienko (CAN) scored three times in just 21 sec to register the **fastest NHL hat-trick**. The Blackhawks had been 6–2 down in the third period – following Mosienko's intervention, they went on to win the game 7–6.

24 MARCH

Aged 18 years 359 days, Colton Herta (USA, b. 30 Mar 2000) became the **youngest winner of an IndyCar race** in 2019. He won the IndyCar Classic at Circuit of the Americas in Austin, Texas – to date, the one and only staging of that race.

25 MARCH

At the 1988 World Figure Skating Championships, Kurt Browning (CAN) performed the **first figure skating quadruple jump**. He successfully landed a toe loop with four airborne rotations during his free skating routine in Budapest, Hungary. Despite his history-making leap, Browning finished the competition in sixth – he would go on, however, to become a four-time men's singles world champion.

26 MARCH

In 2016, professional disc golfer Jennifer Allen (USA) unleashed the **farthest-thrown women's flying disc** at the High Desert Distance Challenge in Primm, Nevada, USA. Her effort flew 173.3 m (568 ft 6 in) – around the length of 1½ American football fields – and was recognized by the World Flying Disc Federation.

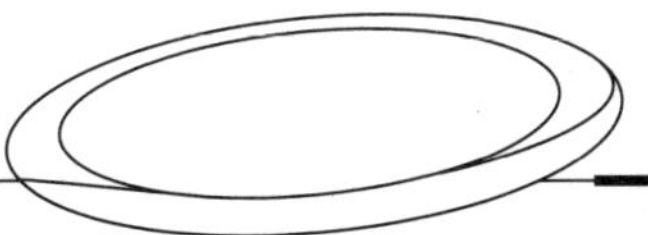

27 MARCH

Freestyle skier Emilie Cruz (FRA) hit 107.14 km/h (66.57 mph) in 2017 while descending the slopes of the French resort of Les Carroz – facing the wrong way! She had been inspired by seeing Elias Ambühl break the men's record for "switch" skiing the previous month. Cruz set the first-ever record for the **fastest women's speed skiing backwards**, which remains unbroken to this day.

> Two years after her first GWR record title, Cruz ditched her skis to earn herself a second. At the Marathon de Genève in Switzerland on 12 May 2019, she completed the **fastest women's half-marathon in ski boots**, in 3 hr 7 min 35 sec.

28 MARCH

The **fastest University Men's Boat Race** took place in 1998, when Cambridge rowed to victory over their old rivals Oxford in 16 min 19 sec. The Light Blues beat the previous record by 26 sec, notching their sixth win in a row. First used in 1845, the Championship Course runs along the River Thames between Putney and Mortlake in London, stretching 4 mi 374 yards (6.8 km) – more than three times the standard distance of Olympic rowing events (2,000 m).

29 MARCH

In 1999, ice hockey legend Wayne Gretzky (CAN) fired home his 894th and final NHL goal during the New York Rangers' 3–1 win over the New York Islanders at Madison Square Garden. "The Great One" – who had previously played for the Edmonton Oilers, the Los Angeles Kings and the St Louis Blues – played his final pro game the following month. He retired having achieved numerous records, including the **most NHL goals**.

30 MARCH

At the 2014 International Table Tennis Federation World Tour German Open, the Japanese pairing of Mima Ito (b. 21 Oct 2000) and Miu Hirano (b. 14 Apr 2000) became the **youngest winners of an ITTF World Tour doubles title**, with a combined age of just 27 years 145 days. Ito was 13 years 160 days old; Hirano 13 years 350 days.

31 MARCH

The **youngest women's tennis No.1** was crowned in 1997: Martina Hingis (CHE, b. 30 Sep 1980), aged 16 years 182 days. The teenage tyro summitted the world rankings after a run of five consecutive tournament wins – including her first Grand Slam singles title, at the 1997 Australian Open, which made her the youngest winner of a major in the 20th century.

> *"With the smile of a cheerleader and the appetite of a shark, Hingis is the epitome of a new wave of tennis teenagers with no qualms about preying on the older generation."*
>
> (*The New York Times*, following Hingis's victory at Wimbledon in 1997)

1 APRIL

At the Brazilian Athletics Challenge event in São Paulo in 2022, para sprinter Petrúcio Ferreira dos Santos (BRA) ran the **fastest men's 200 m (T47)** in 20.83 sec. Dos Santos, who lost his lower left arm after an accident at the age of two, is the fastest Paralympian on the planet, having clocked 10.29 sec for the 100 m at the same event.

2 APRIL

In 1977, thoroughbred steeplechaser Red Rum completed the **most wins of the Grand National by a horse** with his third victory at Aintree Racecourse in Merseyside, UK. The 12-year-old had previously triumphed in 1973 and 1974, finishing second in the two years afterwards.

> *"They say records are there to be broken, but Red Rum's at Aintree is one that will stand the test of time."*
>
> (Tony McCoy, 20-time champion jockey)

3 APRIL

Cambridge recorded the **fastest Women's Boat Race** in 2022, triumphing over Oxford in 18 min 22 sec on the River Thames in London. It was their fifth consecutive win in the annual race, and took their overall record to 46 victories against Oxford's 30.

> **The first Women's Boat Race took place in 1927 on the Isis river in Oxford. Barred from racing side by side, the crews took turns to row a 0.5-mi-long (0.8-km) course upstream and down, and were judged on style as well as speed.**

4 APRIL

In 1997, Dave Pearson (UK) achieved the **fastest time to pot all 15 balls on a US pool table** – clearing up in just 26.5 sec. Pearson, known as the "Ginger Wizard", was playing at Peppers Bar & Grill in Windsor, Ontario, Canada.

5 APRIL

Anat Draigor (ISR) racked up the **most points in a women's basketball game** – 136 – in 2006. The 46-year-old was playing in an Israel Division III League play-off game for Hapoel Mate Yehuda against Elitzur Givat Shmuel. She scored a staggering 86% of her team's final total of 158 points; Hapoel's opponents managed just 41 in reply.

6 APRIL

The **first modern Olympic champion** was crowned in 1896, when James Connolly (USA) won the hop, skip and jump with a 13.71-m (44-ft 11-in) effort in Athens, Greece. He became the first recorded winner at the Games in 1,527 years, since the Armenian boxer Prince Varasdates in 369 CE. Connolly received a silver medal, rather than a gold, for his Olympic victory – along with an olive branch and a diploma.

Connolly had to withdraw from his studies at Harvard University in order to compete at the 1896 Olympics, after being denied a leave of absence. He later became a journalist and a writer. In 1949, Connolly was offered an honorary doctorate by Harvard – which he declined.

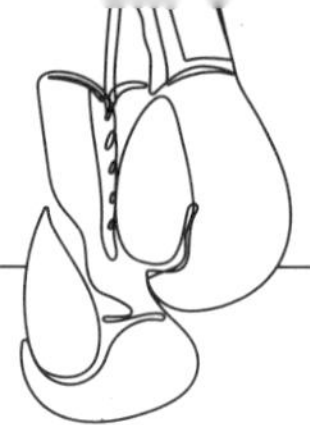

7 APRIL

In 1893, the **longest gloved boxing match** came to a conclusion in New Orleans, Louisiana, USA. The epic bout between Andy Bowen and Jack Burke (both USA) began on 6 Apr at 9:15 p.m. and ended at 4:34 a.m., after a total of 7 hr 19 min and 110 rounds. Despite outlasting the referee – who was changed after Round 93, exhausted – neither combatant could outlast the other. The fight was declared a no contest, later changed to a draw.

8 APRIL

The St Louis Cardinals (USA) displayed their bench strength in 2016 by hitting the **most pinch-hit home runs by a team in an MLB game**. Substitute batters Jeremy Hazelbaker, Aledmys Díaz and Greg Garcia all went deep as the Cardinals beat the Atlanta Braves 7–4 at Turner Field in Georgia, USA. Díaz, a rookie, registered his first-ever Major League dinger.

9 APRIL

In 1988, Southampton striker Alan Shearer (UK, b. 13 Aug 1970) scored three times against Arsenal to become the **youngest hat-trick scorer in English football's top division**, aged 17 years 240 days. He found the net just five minutes into his full debut and completed his hat-trick four minutes after half-time – breaking the 30-year-old record of Chelsea's Jimmy Greaves.

> *"Nobody was as mentally tough as Alan. Probably the greatest Premiership player ever."*
>
> (Michael Owen, former England striker)

10 APRIL

In the first qualifying round of a 2016 tournament in Pelham, Alabama, USA, Gail Falkenberg (USA, b. 16 Jan 1947) became the **oldest match-winner on the International Tennis Federation circuit**, aged 69 years 85 days. She defeated Rosalyn Small, who was 47 years her junior, 6–0, 6–1.

11 APRIL

The **highest score in a men's international football match** occurred in 2001, when Australia thumped American Samoa 31–0 in a FIFA World Cup qualifying game at Coffs Harbour in New South Wales, Australia. Striker Archie Thompson helped himself to the **most individual goals** – 13. "The American Samoa team were absolute beginners," he said, "but we had to show them the respect of trying our best."

Australia 31–0 American Samoa

Boutsianis	10', 50', 84'
Thompson	12', 23', 27', 29', 32', 37', 42' 45', 56', 60', 65', 85', 88'
Zdrilic	13', 21', 25', 33', 58', 66', 78', 89'
A. Vidmar	14', 80'
Popovic	17', 19'
Colosimo	51', 81'
De Amicis	55'

12 APRIL

At golf's 2015 Masters in Augusta, Jordan Spieth (USA) claimed his first major with a dominant wire-to-wire win. He opened with a round of -8 and finished on a record-equalling score of 270 (-18). Spieth also sank the **most birdies at a Masters tournament** – 28.

13 APRIL

Paula Radcliffe (UK) ran the **fastest women's London Marathon** in 2003, crossing the line in 2 hr 15 min 25 sec. She broke her own outright women's marathon world record from the 2002 Chicago Marathon by almost two minutes – setting a mark that would stand for 16 years.

> *"The greatest distance running performance I have seen in my lifetime... it ranks in my mind with Bob Beamon's long jump in 1968."*
>
> (Dave Bedford, London Marathon race director)

14 APRIL

In Game 5 of the 1962 NBA Finals, Elgin Baylor (USA) dropped 61 points for the Los Angeles Lakers as they defeated the Boston Celtics 126–121 at Boston Garden. The Celtics recovered to win the next two games and claim the championship, but Baylor at least had the consolation of the record for the **most points in an NBA Finals game**.

15 APRIL

At the 2005 Audrey Walton Combined Events in Columbia, Missouri, USA, Austra Skujytė (LTU) scored the **most points in a women's decathlon** – 8,358. She competed in 10 events over two days. It was only the second world record recognized by World Athletics in the discipline.

Skujytė's multi-event masterclass

EVENT	MEASUREMENT	EVENT	MEASUREMENT
100 m	12.49 sec	100 m hurdles	14.22 sec
Long jump	6.12 m	Discus throw	46.19 m
Shot put	16.42 m	Pole vault	3.10 m
High jump	1.78 m	Javelin throw	48.78 m
400 m	57.19 sec	1,500 m	5 min 15.86 sec

16 APRIL

The 111th Boston Marathon in 2007 had an unusual entrant – NASA astronaut Sunita Williams (USA), who was competing onboard the *International Space Station*. Williams ran on a treadmill taped with her official bib, numbered 14,000, as she circled Earth at around 17,500 mph (28,163 km/h). Her finishing time of 4 hr 24 min is the **fastest women's marathon in orbit**.

17 APRIL

In 2019, Iker Casillas (ESP) played his 177th and final game in the UEFA Champions League, a 4–1 defeat for his FC Porto side against Liverpool. This is the **most appearances by a goalkeeper** in the competition. The Spanish shot-stopper played in 27 Champions League matches for Porto and 150 for Real Madrid, picking up three winners' medals with the Spanish giants.

18 APRIL

A C Green (USA) played his final regular-season NBA game in 2001, a 103–91 win for the Miami Heat over the Orlando Magic. It signalled the end of an incredible Ironman streak that began on 19 Nov 1986 and saw Green appear in 1,192 matches in a row – the **most consecutive NBA games**. Over the course of his 16-year NBA career, Green missed just three regular-season games.

19 APRIL

In 2014, Bernard Hopkins (USA, b. 15 Jan 1965) outpointed Beibut Shumenov at the DC Armory in Washington, DC, USA, to defend his IBF light heavyweight belt and win the WBA (super) light heavyweight title. At 49 years 94 days, Hopkins became the **oldest men's boxing world champion**. His astonishing longevity in the ring earned him the nickname "The Alien".

20 APRIL

Danica Patrick (USA) became the **first female winner of an IndyCar race** in 2008. She took the checkered flag at the Indy Japan 300 at Twin Ring Motegi. Patrick, who was driving for Andretti Green Racing in her 50th IndyCar start, took the lead on lap 198 of the 200-lap race. To date, she is the only woman to have won in the series.

> *"This is a long time coming. I've been asked so many times when I'm going to win my first race, and finally, no more of those questions."*
>
> (Danica Patrick, on her maiden IndyCar win)

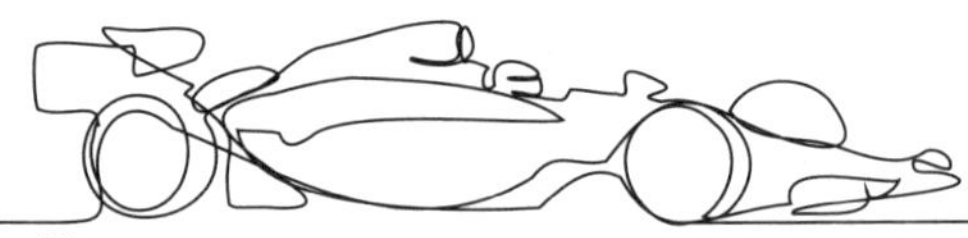

21 APRIL

At the 1997 World Snooker Championship, Ronnie O'Sullivan (UK) made history by compiling the **fastest 147 break** – timed at 5 min 8 sec – at the Crucible Theatre in Sheffield, South Yorkshire, UK. The 21-year-old O'Sullivan completed his lightning-quick 147 during his first-round victory over Mick Price. It was the first of a record 15 maximums that O'Sullivan has made – against 15 different opponents.

During qualifying for the 2017 World Snooker Championship, Fergal O'Brien (IRL) and David Gilbert (UK) contested the **longest professional snooker frame**, lasting 2 hr 3 min 41 sec – three minutes slower than the men's marathon world record, and around 24 times longer than Ronnie O'Sullivan's maximum clearance.

22 APRIL

At the 2022 Zurich Classic of New Orleans in Louisiana, USA, golfer Jay Haas (USA, b. 2 Dec 1953) became the **oldest player to make the cut on the PGA Tour** at the age of 68 years 141 days. He was paired alongside his son, Bill. Jay Haas played 799 PGA Tour events, winning nine and making the **most cuts** – 592.

23 APRIL

Shane Long (IRL) scored the **fastest goal in the English Premier League** in 2019, rifling home after just 7.69 sec for Southampton against Watford at Vicarage Road. Of the 10 quickest strikes in the league to date – all of which were scored in under 14 sec – a total of eight were scored by the away side.

Top 5 EPL fastest scorers

PLAYER	MATCH	DATE	TIME
Shane Long	Watford vs SOUTHAMPTON	23 Apr 2019	7.69 sec
Philip Billing	Arsenal vs BOURNEMOUTH	4 Mar 2023	9.11 sec
Ledley King	Bradford City vs TOTTENHAM	9 Dec 2000	9.82 sec
Abdoulaye Doucouré	EVERTON vs Leicester City	1 Feb 2025	10.18 sec
Alan Shearer	NEWCASTLE vs Manchester City	18 Jan 2003	10.52 sec

24 APRIL

At the 2016 London Marathon, Damian Thacker and Luke Symonds (both UK) ran the **fastest three-legged men's marathon**. The two physiotherapists crossed the line (together) in 3 hr 7 min 57 sec, knocking more than half an hour off the previous record. Victoria Carter and Sarah Dudgeon (both UK) set the matching **women's** record of 3 hr 47 min 19 sec in the same race.

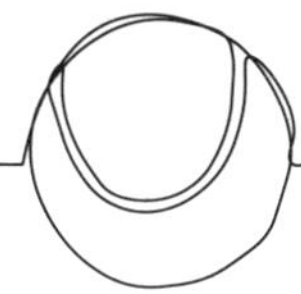

25 APRIL

Tennis player Anna Kournikova (RUS, b. 7 Jun 1981) became the **youngest match-winner at the Billie Jean King Cup** in 1996, beating Anna-Karin Svensson 6–0, 6–3 aged 14 years 323 days. The blue-riband international team competition in women's tennis, the Billie Jean King Cup was launched in 1963 and was known as the Federation or Fed Cup until 2020.

26 APRIL

In 1935, Frank Boucher (CAN) of the New York Rangers won the Lady Byng Trophy for sportsmanship and excellence for the seventh time in eight seasons. The award had been created by the viceregal consort of Canada, a keen ice hockey fan. She donated a second trophy – renamed after her death in 1949 – after giving Boucher the original for good. His record for the **most wins of the Lady Byng Memorial Trophy** still stands.

Frank Boucher's ability to steal the puck from his opponents on the ice earned him the nickname "Raffles", after the fictional gentleman-thief created by author E W Hornung.

27 APRIL

At the 1991 San Marino Grand Prix, McLaren driver Ayrton Senna (BRA) qualified fastest for the seventh year in succession at the Imola Circuit – the **most consecutive pole positions at a Formula One Grand Prix**. The next day, he won the race for the third time. In 1994, Senna claimed his eighth pole in San Marino – during the race itself, however, his car left the track at the Tamburello corner and crashed into a concrete barrier, fatally injuring him.

28 APRIL

In the final of the 2007 Cricket World Cup in Bridgetown, Barbados, wicketkeeper-opener Adam Gilchrist smashed a rapid-fire 149 to help Australia to a 53-run victory over Sri Lanka via the Duckworth/Lewis method. Gilchrist raced to three figures in just 72 balls, making it the **fastest century in a Cricket World Cup final**.

29 APRIL

At 21 years 106 days old, Stephen Hendry (UK, b. 13 Jan 1969) became the **youngest men's snooker world champion** in 1990. He defeated Jimmy White 18–12 in the final, and went on to win six out of the next nine world titles – beating the unfortunate White in the final three more times.

30 APRIL

In 2005, heavy-hitting Christy Martin (USA) took her record for the **most knockouts in women's boxing** to 32, stopping Lana Alexander in the second round in Lula, Mississippi, USA. Martin, a WBC female super welterweight champion and International Boxing Hall of Fame inductee, won 49 of her 59 pro bouts, going unbeaten for eight years between 1990 and 1998. She was the first woman to box on US national and pay-per-view TV.

1 MAY

In 1999, Manuel Schütz (CHE) unleashed the **farthest long distance boomerang throw** in the shadow of Zurich Airport in Switzerland. The mercurial missile travelled 238 m (780 ft 10 in) – more than twice the length of the javelin world record – before returning back to cross the baseline from where "Manu" had delivered it. His Herculean throw was ratified by the International Federation of Boomerang Associations.

> *"A crazy lot of people... Who else would be willing to search for days for a lost boomerang?"*
>
> (Manuel Schütz on long-distance boomerang throwers)

2 MAY

Icelandic strongman Hafþór Júlíus Björnsson achieved the **heaviest deadlift** in 2020, hoisting 501 kg (1,104 lb 8 oz) – heavier than a grand piano – at Thor's Power Gym in Kópavogur, Iceland. Björnsson, who won the World's Strongest Man competition in 2018, found fame on the small screen playing the psychotic knight Gregor "The Mountain" Clegane in HBO's *Game of Thrones*.

3 MAY

In 1992, Geelong racked up the **highest team score in Australian rules football**, mauling the Brisbane Bears by 37.17 (239) to 11.9 (75) at Carrara Oval in Queensland. The Cats kicked 14 goals in the last quarter to break the previous record, 36.22 (238), set by Fitzroy in 1979. Geelong's record haul of 239 points comprised 37 goals (worth six points) and 17 behinds (worth one).

Geelong also played in the game featuring the **lowest team score in Australian rules football**. During their 1899 sectional-round tie at the Corio Oval, they kept St Kilda to a single behind while racking up a then-record total of 23.24 (162) – winning by 161 points. Impressively, it was St Kilda who actually scored first.

4 MAY

In 2022, the No.10 shirt worn by Diego Maradona during Argentina's 1986 World Cup quarter-final with England became the **most expensive football shirt sold at auction**, fetching £7,142,500 ($8.9 m) at Sotheby's in London. Maradona scored twice against England – his infamous "Hand of God" goal, when he appeared to punch the ball into the net, followed by a mesmerizing dribble past four defenders that was voted the "Goal of the Century" in a 2002 FIFA poll.

5 MAY

The **fastest time for the Kentucky Derby** was set in 1973 by the legendary Secretariat, who galloped around the 1¼-mi (2,012-m) course at Churchill Downs in Louisville, Kentucky, USA, in 1 min 59.4 sec. He was ridden by Canadian jockey Ron Turcotte.

In 1973, Secretariat claimed the Triple Crown by winning three classic US races for three-year-old thoroughbred horses: the Kentucky Derby, Preakness Stakes and Belmont Stakes. Secretariat still holds the fastest winning time for all three races, more than 50 years later.

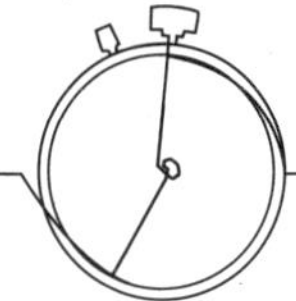

6 MAY

In 1954, medical student Roger Bannister (UK) smashed through one of the great sporting barriers when he completed the **first sub-four-minute mile** at the Iffley Road track in Oxford, UK. He crossed the line in 3 min 59.4 sec, watched by track announcer Norris McWhirter – who, together with his twin Ross, would compile the first edition of *The Guinness Book of Records*.

> *"I leapt at the tape... My effort was over and I collapsed almost unconscious. I felt like an exploded flashlight. I knew that I had done it before I even heard the time."*
>
> (Roger Bannister)

7 MAY

Flying winger Chris Ashton (UK) scored his 41st try in the European Rugby Champions Cup during Leicester's 23–14 quarter-final loss to Leinster in 2022. He had previously scored eight for Northampton Saints, 29 for Saracens, two for French side Toulon and one for Sale. This is the **most European Rugby Champions Cup tries**.

8 MAY

In 2020, Gui Khury (BRA) landed the **first skateboard 1,080 on a vert ramp**, completing three full 360° rotations while airborne in Curitiba, Brazil. He made skateboarding history at the age of just 11. The trick had been successfully performed by Tom Schaar back in 2012, albeit with the aid of a "mega ramp" to help him build up speed.

9 MAY

During an ATP Challenger event in 2012 in Busan, South Korea, Sam Groth (AUS) produced the **fastest men's tennis serve** – timed at 263 km/h (163.4 mph). The 1.94-m-tall (6-ft 4-in) right-hander aced the point but lost the match against Uladzimir Ignatik 6–4, 6–3.

10 MAY

In 2016, the Golden State Warriors' Stephen Curry (USA) became the **first unanimous winner of the National Basketball Association's MVP award**, sweeping all 131 first-place votes. Curry averaged more than 30 points a game, sank a record 402 three-pointers and led the Warriors to a record 73 wins in 82 games.

Most NBA MVP awards

PLAYER	TEAM(S)	WINS	YEARS
Kareem Abdul-Jabbar	Milwaukee Bucks, LA Lakers	6	1971–72, 1974, 1976–77, 1980
Bill Russell	Boston Celtics	5	1958, 1961–63, 1965
Michael Jordan	Chicago Bulls	5	1988, 1991–92, 1996, 1998
Wilt Chamberlain	Philadelphia Warriors/76ers	4	1960, 1966–68
LeBron James	Cleveland Cavaliers, Miami Heat	4	2009–10, 2012–13

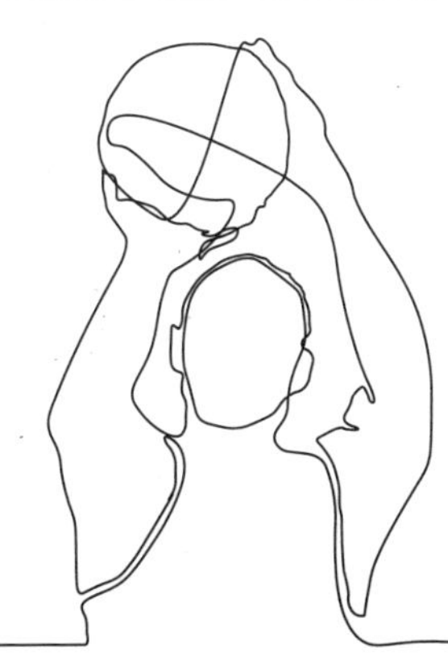

11 MAY

Pitcher Max Scherzer (USA) of the Washington Nationals equalled the record for the **most strikeouts in an MLB game** in 2016, fanning 20 batters from the Detroit Tigers. He threw 96 of his 119 pitches for strikes. Scherzer matched the nine-innings feats of Kerry Wood in 1998 and Roger Clemens (both USA), twice, in 1986 and 1996.

Tom Cheney (USA) of the Washington Senators pitched 21 strikeouts against the Baltimore Orioles on 12 Sep 1962 – but the game went to 16 innings, disqualifying him from the official nine-innings record.

12 MAY

In 2021, goalkeeper Gianluigi Buffon (ITA) made his final Italian league appearance during Juventus's 3–1 win over Sassuolo. The 43-year-old signed off in style, saving a first-half penalty. Buffon had made his Serie A debut as a 17-year-old for Parma back in 1995. He went on to win a record 10 Italian championships and make the **most Serie A appearances**, playing a total of 657 games.

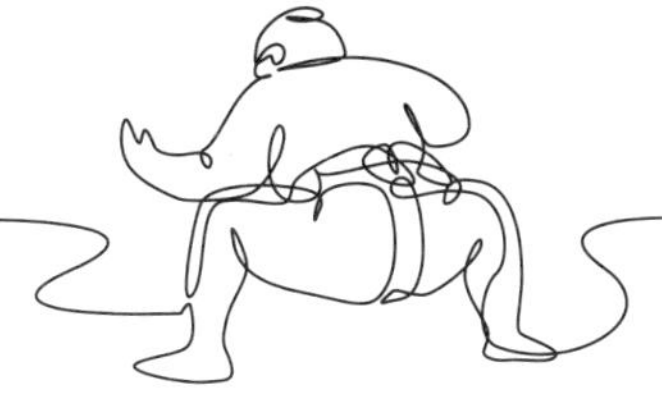

13 MAY

At the 2000 Summer Tournament, sumo wrestler Asanokiri (JPN) was disqualified from his bout against Chiyohakuho on account of his *mawashi* (belt) becoming unravelled, loosening his loincloth – live on Japanese television. The embarrassing uniform slip was the first time in 83 years that a fight had been decided in such a fashion, making it the **rarest loss in sumo**.

14 MAY

In 2016, Gabriel Medina (BRA) landed the **first surfing backflip in competition**, going head over heels at the Oi Rio Pro in Rio de Janeiro, Brazil. He received a perfect score of 10 from the judges for his ground-breaking move.

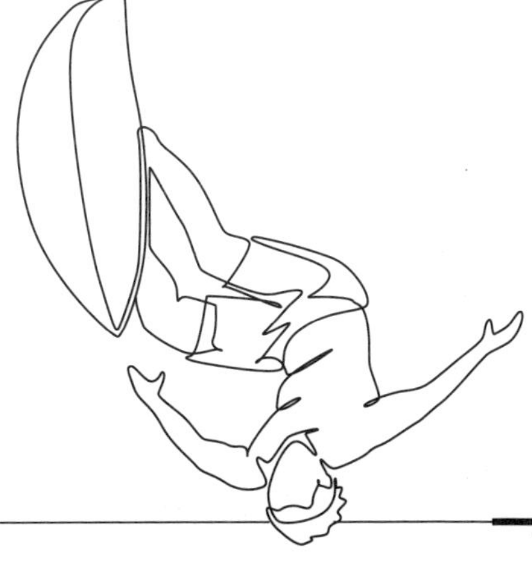

15 MAY

The 2016 Spanish Grand Prix at the Circuit de Barcelona-Catalunya was won by up-and-coming driver Max Verstappen (NLD, b. BEL, 30 Sep 1997) in his first race for the Red Bull team. Verstappen, who had just switched seats from Toro Rosso, became the **youngest driver to win a Formula One Grand Prix**, aged 18 years 228 days.

Youngest F1 race winners

DRIVER	TEAM	GRAND PRIX	AGE
Max Verstappen	Red Bull	Spain 2016	18 years 228 days
Sebastian Vettel	Toro Rosso	Italy 2008	21 years 73 days
Charles Leclerc	Ferrari	Belgium 2019	21 years 320 days
Fernando Alonso	Renault	Hungary 2003	22 years 26 days
Troy Ruttman	Kuzma	Indianapolis 1952	22 years 80 days

16 MAY

Katie Ledecky (USA) swam the **fastest women's 1,500 m freestyle** – 15 min 20.48 sec – at the 2018 TYR Pro Swim Series meet in Indianapolis, Indiana, USA. This is 18 sec quicker than anyone else in history. Ledecky currently owns the fastest 20 times in the long course event, which comprises 30 lengths of an Olympic-sized swimming pool and measures almost a mile in length.

17 MAY

John Kelly (USA) reclaimed his record for the **fastest ultrarun of the Pennine Way** in 2021, running the length of Great Britain's oldest National Trail in 58 hr 4 min. Stretching for 268 mi (431 km) between the Scottish Borders and Derbyshire, the Pennine Way is a gruelling endurance challenge, complete with mud, peat bogs and a vertical gain of almost 12,000 m (39,000 ft). Kelly slept for "around 20 minutes" over the course of his three-day odyssey.

18 MAY

In 1968, Frank Howard of the Washington Senators (USA) hit two dingers against the Detroit Tigers to complete the **most MLB home runs in a week**. The imposing 2-m-tall (6-ft 7-in) slugger, nicknamed "The Capital Punisher" and "The Washington Monument", went deep 10 times in 20 at-bats over seven days.

19 MAY

The **quickest badminton match** took place at the 1996 Uber Cup – also known as the World Women's Team Championships – in Hong Kong, China. Ra Kyung-min (KOR) took just 6 min to dispose of England's Julia Mann by a score of 11–2, 11–1.

> **In May 2023, a badminton doubles match between Malaysia's Pearly Tan and Thinaah Muralitharan and Japan's Rena Miyaura and Ayako Sakuramoto hit the headlines thanks to a rally lasting 211 shots. The epic exchange went on for more than three minutes – half the time that it took Ra Kyung-min to win her entire match against Julia Mann.**

20 MAY

In 2010, freestyler Abraham Muñoz (MEX) finally called time on his record attempt for the **longest time continuously controlling a football**, having kept the ball off the ground for 21 hr 1 min in New York City. He rested it on his neck during breaks between keepie-uppies.

21 MAY

Scuderia Ferrari made their Formula One debut at the 1950 Monaco Grand Prix, recording second- and fourth-place finishes for drivers Alberto Ascari and Raymond Sommer. On a chaotic first lap, the track at Tabac Corner was flooded by a harbour wave, causing a pile-up that led to nine of the 19 entrants retiring from the race. Ferrari have since gone on to make the **most Formula One starts by a constructor** – 1,098, as of the end of the 2024 season.

A deeply superstitious man, Alberto Ascari feared black cats and unlucky numbers and always raced in his lucky blue helmet and the same T-shirt, gloves and goggles. In 1955, Ascari took part in an impromptu testing session at Monza, wearing his own jacket and tie and a borrowed helmet. He suffered an unexplained crash on the third lap and died from his injuries.

22 MAY

The **first women's Olympic champion** was crowned in 1900, when Hélène de Pourtalès (CHE, b. Helen Barbey, USA) was a member of the winning crew in the 1–2 ton sailing event at Meulan-en-Yvelines in France. She sailed with her husband and nephew onboard the *Lérina*. Women had been barred from competing at the first modern Olympics in 1896 and were permitted to take part in just five sports in Paris: croquet, equestrianism, golf, sailing and tennis. They would not be allowed to enter the athletics events until the Amsterdam Games in 1928.

Female gold medallists at the 1900 Olympics

SPORT	EVENT	CHAMPION
Sailing	1-2 ton	Hélène de Pourtalès*
Tennis	Women's singles	Charlotte Cooper (UK)
	Mixed doubles	Charlotte Cooper**
Golf	Women's individual	Margaret Abbott (USA)

**with Hermann and Bernard de Pourtalès*

***with Reginald Doherty*

23 MAY

Phil Mickelson (USA, b. 16 Jun 1970) became the **oldest winner of a major golf tournament** in 160 years when he claimed the 2021 PGA Championship at the age of 50 years 341 days. He had been ranked 115th in the world going into the tournament, which was staged at Kiawah Island in South Carolina, USA. "Lefty" had earned the first of his 45 wins on the PGA Tour 30 years earlier.

24 MAY

Ajax defeated AC Milan 1–0 in the final of the 1995 UEFA Champions League, staged at the Ernst Happel Stadium in the Austrian capital of Vienna. The 85th-min winner was hit by substitute striker Patrick Kluivert (NLD, b. 1 Jul 1976), who was 18 years 327 days old. He remains the **youngest goal scorer in a UEFA Champions League final**.

25 MAY

At the 1935 Big Ten Championships in Ann Arbor, Michigan, USA, athlete Jesse Owens (USA) produced one of the greatest sporting displays in history, setting six world records in just 45 min. He was not even fully fit, having injured his back falling down stairs five days earlier. Owens only had time for one effort in the long jump, but his mark of 8.13 m (26 ft 8 in) remained the world record for 25 years. His record for the **most athletics world records in one day** will likely never be equalled.

Jesse Owens' Finest Hour

TIME	EVENT	RECORD
3.15 p.m.	100 yard dash	9.4 sec*
3.25 p.m.	Long jump	8.13 m
3.34 p.m.	220 yard dash	20.3 sec
	200 m dash	20.3 sec
4.00 p.m.	220 yard low hurdles	22.6 sec
	200 m low hurdles	22.6 sec

**tied the world record*

26 MAY

In 2019, former tennis pro Trent Hayward (USA) fired down the **most successful tennis serves in one hour** – 1,658 – in Flagstaff, Arizona, USA. That's more than one every two seconds. Hayward overcame 40-mph (64-km/h) gusts of wind to break a record that had stood for eight years.

27 MAY

Ryan Crouser (USA) launched the **farthest men's shot put** in 2023, sending it 23.56 m (77 ft 3 in) at Los Angeles' Drake Stadium. The 2.01-m-tall (6-ft 7-in) Olympic champion showcased a new technique – dubbed the "Crouser Slide" – which added a step to his approach inside the circle, enabling Crouser to generate more speed and power.

Crouser defended his Olympic title at the 2020 Games, with Joe Kovacs taking silver and Tomas Walsh the bronze. This was an exact repeat of the podium placings at Rio 2016 – the first time that this had happened in an individual event in the 125-year history of the modern Olympics.

28 MAY

The first Isle of Man TT motorcycle race took place in 1907. Charles Collier won the single-cylinder class, completing 10 laps of the 15.81-mi (25.44-km) circuit of public roads in 4 hr 8 min, at an average speed of 38.21 mph (61.49 km/h). Harry Rembrandt "Rem" Fowler won the twin-cylinder class. Still contested 118 years later, the Isle of Man TT is the **oldest annual motorcycle race**.

> *"I had to make up my mind whether to stop or plunge blind through a wall of fire which stretched right across the road at the Devil's Elbow... I shall never forget the hot blast of those flames."*
>
> (Rem Fowler)

29 MAY

During Castleford Tigers' match against Leigh Centurions in 2017, rugby league star Greg Eden (UK) scored the **fastest Super League hat-trick**, touching down three times in just 4 min 59 sec. It was the fourth consecutive league game in which Eden had scored a hat-trick.

30 MAY

In 1911, racing driver Ray Harroun (USA) became the **first winner of the Indianapolis 500** – then named the "International Sweepstakes". Behind the wheel of his Marmon Wasp, Harroun hurtled round 200 laps of the Indianapolis Motor Speedway in 6 hr 42 min 8 sec, at an average speed of 74 mph (120 km/h). His Wasp boasted the first rear-view mirror used in racing.

31 MAY

In 1970, the **first yellow card at the FIFA World Cup** was shown by referee Kurt Tschenscher to Soviet Union midfielder Kakhi Asatiani after half an hour of their 0–0 draw against hosts Mexico. Although referees had previously been able to caution players and expel them from the field of play, this was the first time that physical cards had been produced in the history of sport.

The same match also saw the first World Cup substitution, with the Soviet Union's Anatoliy Puzach, a striker, replacing midfielder Viktor Serebryanikov during the half-time interval.

1 JUNE

In the final of the 1997 IBF World Championships in Glasgow, UK, Peter Rasmussen (DNK) and Sun Jun (CHN) contested the **longest badminton singles match**, battling it out for 2 hr 4 min. It was the Dane who eventually prevailed, 16–17, 18–13, 15–10. Sun had been just two points from victory in the second game – in the third, he suffered severe cramps as the marathon match took its toll.

2 JUNE

Tunisia became the **first African team to win a game at the FIFA World Cup** in 1978, defeating Mexico 3–1 in a Group 2 encounter at the Estadio Gigante de Arroyito in Rosario, Argentina. They were only the fourth side from the continent to qualify for the finals, after Egypt in 1934, Morocco in 1970 and Zaire (now the Democratic Republic of the Congo) in 1974.

3 JUNE

In 2017, Alex Honnold (USA) completed the **first free solo climb of El Capitan**, scaling the 7,569-ft-high (2,307-m) monolith in California's Yosemite National Park in 3 hr 56 min without using ropes, harnesses or other protective gear. Honnold's daredevil ascent, the culmination of an eight-year quest, was captured in the Oscar-winning documentary *Free Solo* (USA, 2018).

> *"We are apes – we should be climbing."*
>
> (Alex Honnold)

4 JUNE

In 1995, New Zealand racked up the **highest score at the Rugby World Cup**, shellacking Japan 145–17 in Bloemfontein, South Africa. The All Blacks ran in 21 tries, with Marc Ellis touching down six times. Simon Culhane scored 45 points on his Test debut, making 20 of 21 conversions and going over for a try. But his record haul was in vain – Culhane was dropped for first-choice fly-half Andrew Mehrtens for New Zealand's next game, and won only a further five caps.

5 JUNE

In the final of the 2022 French Open, Rafael Nadal (ESP) defeated Norway's Casper Ruud 6–3, 6–3, 6–0 to extend his record for the **most wins of a Grand Slam singles tennis tournament** to 14. The "King of Clay" claimed his first major at Roland Garros in 2005 and went on to compile an astonishing record of 112 wins and four losses from 116 matches at the French Open. His closest rival is Margaret Court, who won 11 Australian Open titles between 1960 and 1973.

Rafa's French Open reverses

YEAR	ROUND	OPPONENT	SCORE
2009	4	Robin Söderling (SWE)	2–6, 7–6, 4–6, 6–7
2015	QF	Novak Djokovic (SRB)	5–7, 3–6, 1–6
2021	SF	Novak Djokovic	6–3, 3–6, 6–7, 2–6
2024	1	Alexander Zverev (DEU)	3–6, 6–7, 3–6

6 JUNE

Warwickshire batsman Brian Lara (TTO) completed the **highest innings in a men's first-class cricket match** in 1994, finishing on 501 not out in an English County Championship fixture against Durham at Edgbaston. His 7-hr 54-min knock – which had started three days earlier – contained 62 fours and 10 sixes. Lara scored 390 runs on 6 Jun alone. He had been bowled by a no-ball and dropped by the Durham wicketkeeper before he reached 20.

7 JUNE

Brothers Ben and Tom Birchall (both UK) recorded the **fastest sidecar lap at the Isle of Man TT races** in 2023, completing the course in 18 min 45.850 sec, at an average speed of 120.645 mph (194.159 km/h) in their Honda LCR. The Birchall brothers became the first sidecar racers to break the 120-mph barrier, on the 100th anniversary of the event's debut at the Isle of Man TT.

8 JUNE

In 2009, freediver Stéphane Mifsud (FRA) held his breath while floating face-down in a swimming pool for 11 min 35 sec in Hyères, France. The lung-busting feat – the **longest-duration static apnea** – was ratified by the AIDA freediving federation. Mifsud can slow his heart rate down to fewer than 20 beats per minute.

> *"I grew up on Réunion Island, where my father introduced me to the sea. This is how my passion for freediving was born."*
>
> (Stéphane Mifsud)

9 JUNE

Cyclist Eddy Merckx (BEL) won the 1973 Giro d'Italia having worn the *maglia ciclamino* (mauve jersey) as leader of the points classification through all 20 stages of the race. It was a fourth successive victory for Merckx – nicknamed "The Cannibal" – at one of the three major European stage cycling races known collectively as the "Grand Tour": the Giro, Vuelta a España and Tour de France. This is the **most consecutive cycling Grand Tour wins**.

10 JUNE

In 1944, Joe Nuxhall (USA, b. 30 Jul 1928) became the **youngest MLB player** when he pitched 2/3 of an inning for the Cincinnati Reds against the St Louis Cardinals aged 15 years 316 days. The game, at Ohio's Crosley Field, took place four days after the D-Day invasion in Europe, leaving Major League teams depleted by the draft. Nuxhall didn't play again in the National League for another eight years.

11 JUNE

The USA achieved the **highest margin of victory in a FIFA Women's World Cup match** in 2019, thumping Thailand 13–0 in Reims, France. Striker Alex Morgan scored five times, equalling the single-game tournament record of her compatriot Michelle Akers, against Chinese Taipei in 1991. Ten of the USA's goals came in the second half.

12 JUNE

At 16 years 118 days old, Josh Pierson (USA, b. 14 Feb 2006) became the **youngest person to finish the 24 Hours of Le Mans** in its 99-year history in 2022. The tyre-screeching tyro had been driving since the age of two, when he first climbed into a kart. Together with United Autosports teammates Alex Lynn and Oliver Jarvis, Pierson steered their #23 ORECA 07 to a 10th-place finish overall.

The **greatest distance covered in the 24 Hours of Le Mans** is 5,410 km (3,362 mi) – farther than from New York City to Los Angeles – by the team of Mike Rockenfeller, Timo Bernhard and Romain Dumas in the Audi R15 TDI Plus in 2010.

13 JUNE

Cricketer Amelia Kerr smashed the **highest innings in a women's One-Day International** – 232 not out – for New Zealand against Ireland in 2018. She hit 31 fours and two sixes, and followed up by taking five Irish wickets. Aged 17 years 243 days, Kerr (b. 13 Oct 2000) became the youngest double centurion in any form of senior international cricket.

14 JUNE

During Game 6 of the 1998 NBA Finals between the Chicago Bulls and the Utah Jazz, Michael Jordan (USA) hit a jump shot with 5.2 sec left on the clock to seal an 87–86 win for the Bulls – clinching the championship by 4 games to 2. Jordan extended his record for the **most NBA Finals MVP awards** to six, all of which he had earned while playing for Chicago.

Game 6 of the 1998 NBA Finals remains the most watched basketball match in US TV history, drawing an audience of 35.8 million. Michael Jordan's series-clinching jump shot was his last for the Chicago Bulls: the six-time champion retired afterwards, although he did return to the NBA with the Washington Wizards in 2001–03.

15 JUNE

Albania scored the **fastest goal at the UEFA European Championships** during their 2024 group match against Italy, Nedim Bajrami lashing home after just 23 sec in Dortmund, Germany. The Eagles were unable to hold on to their lead, however, eventually going down 2–1. The 2024 Euros was notable for its fast starts, with efforts from Türkiye's Merih Demiral, Belgium's Youri Tielemans and Georgia's Khvicha Kvaratskhelia all coming within the first 100 sec.

16 JUNE

Monica Abbott (USA) threw the **fastest softball pitch** in 2012, hitting 77 mph (123.9 km/h). She was playing in a National Pro Fastpitch game for the Chicago Bandits against the Carolina Diamonds in Kannapolis, North Carolina, USA.

17 JUNE

The **first motor racing circuit**, Brooklands, was opened in 1907 in Weybridge, Surrey, UK. Its track was steeply banked and laid with uncoated concrete. The cost was equivalent to around £16 m ($20 m) today. Brooklands played host to the first-ever British Grand Prix in 1926, a 110-lap race stretching 462 km (287 mi).

18 JUNE

At the 2000 US Open in Pebble Beach, California, Tiger Woods (USA) claimed his third major title with a performance that would go down in golfing lore. The 24-year-old obliterated the competition, shooting 65–69–71–67 (272) to finish on 12 under par – a staggering 15 strokes clear of his nearest rival. This is the **largest margin of victory in a golf major championship**.

> *"The greatest performance in golf of all time."*
>
> (*Phil Mickelson on Tiger Woods's 2000 US Open triumph*)

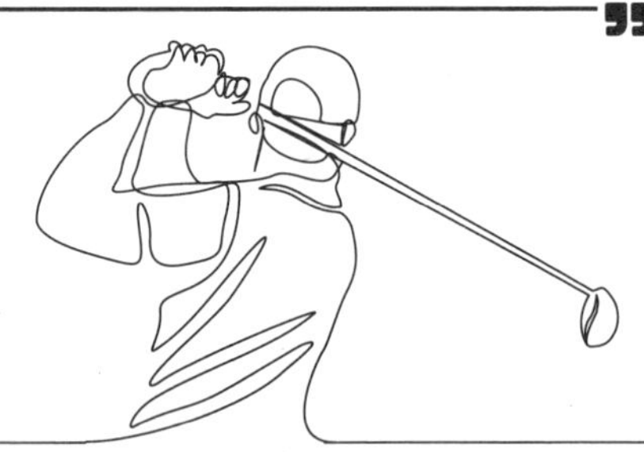

19 JUNE

Brazil's quarter-final match against Wales at the 1958 FIFA World Cup was settled by a strike from their teenage sensation Pelé (BRA, b. Edson Arantes do Nascimento, 23 Oct 1940) at the Ullevi stadium in Gothenburg, Sweden. Aged 17 years 239 days, Pelé became the **youngest goal scorer at the FIFA World Cup**. He went on to score a hat-trick in the semi-final and a brace in the final, claiming the first of his three World Cup winner's medals.

Pelé's World Cup goals

GOAL	CUP	ROUND	OPPONENT	LOCATION
1	1958	QF	Wales	Gothenburg, Sweden
2		SF	France	Solna, Sweden
3			France	
4			France	
5		Final	Sweden	Solna, Sweden
6			Sweden	
7	1962	Group Stage	Mexico	Viña del Mar, Chile
8	1966	Group Stage	Bulgaria	Liverpool, UK
9	1970	Group Stage	Czechoslovakia	Guadalajara, Mexico
10		Group Stage	Romania	Guadalajara, Mexico
11			Romania	
12		Final	Italy	Mexico City, Mexico

20 JUNE

At Pogopalooza 2024 in Pittsburgh, Pennsylvania, USA, Duncan Murray (CAN) performed the **longest jump on a pogo stick** – bounding a vertical distance of 7.15 m (23 ft 5 in) in a single leap. Murray has performed on both *Canada's* and *Britain's Got Talent*.

21 JUNE

In 2021, pitcher Yu Darvish (JPN) of the San Diego Padres fanned 11 Los Angeles Dodgers batters to reach 1,500 career MLB strikeouts. He achieved the milestone in his 197th match – the **fewest MLB games to reach 1,500 career strikeouts**. Darvish eclipsed Randy Johnson's previous record of 206 by nine games.

22 JUNE

In 1937, Joe Louis (USA) knocked out James J Braddock to claim the world heavyweight boxing championship. Louis, nicknamed the "Brown Bomber", reigned until his retirement on 1 Mar 1949 – a total of 11 years 252 days. The **longest-reigning boxing world champion**, his total of 25 consecutive title defences has never been surpassed.

23 JUNE

The **oldest player at a FIFA Women's World Cup** took to the field in 2019 – Brazil's Formiga (b. Miraildes Maciel Mota, 3 Mar 1978), aged 41 years 112 days. The midfielder, who earned the nickname "Ant" for her unselfish teamwork, is the only footballer to have played at seven FIFA World Cups. She made her tournament debut in 1995 at the age of 17.

24 JUNE

At the 2010 Wimbledon Championships, the first-round tie between John Isner (USA) and Nicolas Mahut (FRA) finally came to an end as the American prevailed 70–68 in the fifth set. The titanic tussle had lasted for a total of 11 hr 5 min across three days and is the **longest professional tennis match**. The fifth set alone took 8 hr 11 min – more than the entirety of the previous longest match.

Isner and Mahut didn't have to wait long for a rematch on the grass at SW19. They were drawn together in the first round of the very next Wimbledon in 2011 – this time, however, Isner won in straight sets.

25 JUNE

Justin Seers (AUS) became the **first X Games gold medallist** in 1995. He won the Barefoot Jumping waterski competition in Providence, Rhode Island, USA, beating four-time world champion Ron Scarpa in the final. Other events featured at the inaugural X Games included bungee jumping, street luge, aggressive inline skating and skysurfing.

26 JUNE

Staged on the Great Sound in Bermuda, the 35th America's Cup yacht race in 2017 was won by Emirates Team New Zealand, who coasted to a 7–1 victory over Oracle Team USA. Peter Burling (NZ, b. 1 Jan 1991) became the **youngest helmsman to win the America's Cup**, aged 26 years 176 days.

> The first America's Cup race took place on 22 Aug 1851 around the Isle of Wight in the UK. Queen Victoria was among the spectators who witnessed the New York Yacht Club's schooner *America* finish ahead of 14 vessels from the Royal Yacht Squadron. Originally known as the Hundred Guinea Cup, the trophy would go on to take its name from the winning yacht.

27 JUNE

Skateboard legend Tony Hawk (USA) made history at X Games V in 1999, landing the **first 900 on a skateboard** in San Francisco, California, USA. He completed two-and-a-half airborne rotations at the 11th attempt during the Skateboard Vert Best Trick competition. In 2016, seventeen years later to the day, Hawk successfully performed the trick again at the age of 48.

28 JUNE

At USA '94, Russia defeated Cameroon 6–1, with striker Oleg Salenko helping himself to the **most goals in a FIFA World Cup match** – five. Despite finishing the tournament with a share of the Golden Shoe, the match proved to be Salenko's ninth and final international cap. Cameroon's consolation was scored by evergreen striker Roger Milla (b. 20 May 1952), who at the age of 42 years 39 days became the **oldest goal scorer at the FIFA World Cup**.

29 JUNE

In 2018, a Porsche 919 Hybrid Evo prototype steered by racing driver Timo Bernhard (DEU) completed the **fastest lap of the Nürburgring Nordschleife**, flying round the 12.93-mi (20.8-km) circuit in Germany at an average speed of 233.8 km/h (145.3 mph). Bernhard crossed the finish line in 5 min 19.546 sec, smashing Stefan Bellof's 35-year-old lap record by more than 50 sec..

Situated in the dense forest of the Eifel mountains, the North Loop of the Nürburgring is notorious for its blind corners, elevation changes and variable weather. The circuit was memorably dubbed the "Green Hell" by F1 driver Jackie Stewart after he won the 1968 German Grand Prix in wet and foggy conditions.

30 JUNE

Mia Kretzer (AUS, b 5 Oct 2014) became the **youngest X Games gold medallist** in 2024, aged just 9 years 269 days. The youngest competitor in tournament history, Kretzer landed a 720 to win the Women's Skateboard Vert Best Trick event in Ventura, California, USA.

1 JULY

The **fastest time at the Wife-Carrying World Championships** was set in 2006 in Sonkajärvi, Finland, when Margo Uusorg hefted Sandra Kullas (both EST) along the 253-m (830-ft) obstacle course in 56.9 sec. Entrants for the event do not have to be married; a minimum weight for the "wife" was introduced in 2002.

2 JULY

In 2013, Orica-GreenEDGE (AUS) zoomed to the **fastest team time trial at the Tour de France**. They completed the 25-km (15-mi) stage in Nice in 25 min 56 sec, clocking an average speed of 57.84 km/h (35.94 mph). Orica-GreenEDGE rider Simon Gerrans leapt to the top of the general classification, becoming only the sixth Australian to wear the yellow jersey.

> *"We're a bunch of friends in the team, we've known each other for a long time. So this [yellow] jersey is for the team as well."*
>
> (Simon Gerrans)

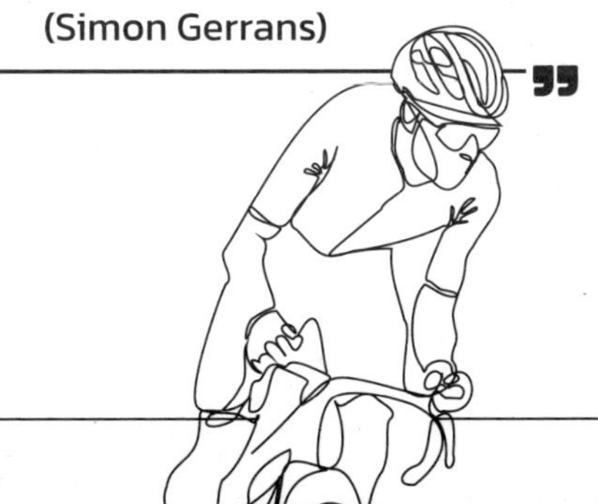

3 JULY

Australia opener Aaron Finch bludgeoned the **highest innings in a men's T20 International** against Zimbabwe in 2018. He reached 172 from just 76 balls, smashing 16 fours and 10 sixes. Finch accounted for 75% of his side's total of 229 at Harare Sports Club in Zimbabwe.

4 JULY

At the 1912 Olympic Games in Stockholm, Sweden, marksman Oscar Swahn (SWE, b. 20 Oct 1847) became the **oldest Olympic gold medallist** at the age of 64 years 258 days. He was part of Sweden's victorious team in the men's 100 m running deer (single shots) – a shooting event where competitors took aim at a moving target. Incredibly, Swahn would go on to win another Olympic medal, a silver, eight years later at the 1920 Antwerp Games.

5 JULY

The USA lifted the FIFA Women's World Cup in 2015 following a 5–2 victory over Japan at BC Place in Vancouver, Canada. Striker Carli Lloyd scored three times in the opening 16 min, completing her hat-trick with a remarkable effort from the halfway line. Lloyd became only the second player – after England's Geoff Hurst in 1966 – to hit a hat-trick in a World Cup final, and claimed the record for the **most goals in a FIFA Women's World Cup final**.

6 JULY

The ladies' title at the 1887 Wimbledon Championships was claimed by schoolgirl Charlotte "Lottie" Dod (UK, b. 24 Sep 1871), who was just 15 years 285 days old. Dod, nicknamed "the Little Wonder", thrashed defending champion Blanche Bingley in the final 6–2, 6–0. The second set lasted just 10 min. Dod remains the **youngest winner of a Grand Slam tennis singles title**.

Lottie Dod is one of sport's greatest all-round athletes. Beyond her success on the tennis court, she played international hockey, won golf's British Ladies Amateur Golf Championship and claimed an Olympic silver medal in archery. She was also the first woman ever to toboggan down the famous Cresta Run ice track in Switzerland.

7 JULY

In 1999, Moroccan athlete Hicham El Guerrouj ran the **fastest men's one mile** – 3 min 43.13 sec – at the Stadio Olimpico in Rome, Italy. He finished ahead of Kenya's Noah Ngeny, who also went below the previous record. To date, neither men's time has been bettered, more than a quarter of a century later.

8 JULY

Kim Sei-young (KOR) tore up the golfing record books at the 2018 Thornberry Creek LPGA Classic in Oneida, Wisconsin, USA. She sank a tour-record 31 birdies in 72 holes to finish the tournament on -31 – the **lowest score to par at an LPGA event**.

9 JULY

In 2017, Sean Maddocks (UK, b. 10 Apr 2002) became the **youngest snooker player to make a 147 break** at the age of 15 years 90 days. The potting prodigy compiled his maximum during a Pro-Am Series match against Jake Nicholson in Leeds, UK. Maddocks claimed the record by eight days from none other than Ronnie O'Sullivan.

10 JULY

Wheelchair tennis player Shingo Kunieda (JPN) claimed his 50th and final Grand Slam title at Wimbledon in 2022, overcoming Alfie Hewett in the final 4–6, 7–5, 7–6. It was Kunieda's first singles title on the grass in London, which only began hosting wheelchair singles events in 2016. He announced his retirement the following year, having claimed the **most Grand Slam wheelchair tennis titles**: an extraordinary 28 in singles and 22 in doubles.

11 JULY

In 1947, Albert Bourlon (FRA) embarked on the **longest post-war Tour de France solo escape**, bursting clear from the peloton and cycling 253 km (157 mi) on his own to win the stage between Carcassonne and Luchon. He finished more than 16 min clear of the field to record his one and only stage win on the Tour.

During World War II, Albert Bourlon won the 1944 Bucharest–Ploieşti–Bucharest classic cycle race while a fugitive from a German PoW camp.

12 JULY

Bowler James Anderson (UK) called time on his Test career in 2024 following England's innings victory over the West Indies at Lord's. The 41-year-old finished the match with four wickets to take his total to 704 – the **most Test wickets by a fast bowler**. Anderson took 123 wickets at Lord's alone, the most by any pace bowler at a single venue.

13 JULY

The **first FIFA World Cup tournament** kicked off in Uruguay in 1930. Thirteen nations contested the event – Egypt were a last-minute withdrawal after bad weather caused them to miss their boat to South America. The tournament opened with a 4–1 win for France over Mexico, Lucien Laurent scoring the first-ever World Cup goal. Hosts Uruguay went on to lift the trophy, beating Argentina 4–2 in the final on 30 Jul.

During the USA's 6–1 semi-final defeat to Argentina at the 1930 FIFA World Cup, physio Jack Coll had to be stretchered from the pitch after accidentally breaking his own bottle of chloroform and knocking himself out with the fumes.

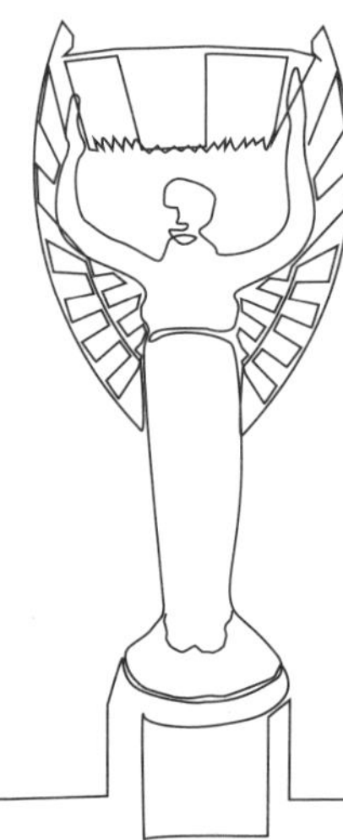

14 JULY

The 2019 Cricket World Cup final was decided in dramatic fashion when England and New Zealand both finished their 50-over innings on 241. An additional "super over" was used to decide the winner – with both sides again tied, this time on 15, England were declared champions thanks to their superior boundary count (26, to the Black Caps' 17). It was the **first Cricket World Cup final won after a super over**.

> *"Two to win. Guptill's going to push for two. They've got to go. It's got... the throw's got to go to the keeper's end... He's got it! England have won the World Cup! By the barest of margins! By the barest of all margins!"*
>
> (New Zealand commentator Ian Smith)

15 JULY

Skateboarder Bob Burnquist (BRA) took to the X Games ramp for the final time in 2017, having competed at every tournament since its first edition in 1995. Burnquist won the **most X Games medals** – 30, including 14 golds. His most famous victory came courtesy of a jaw-dropping Skateboard Vert gold-medal run in 2001, which scored 98.00 and was described by Tony Hawk as the "best vert run we've ever seen".

16 JULY

At the 1988 US Olympic Trials, Florence Griffith-Joyner ran the **fastest women's 100 m** in history, crossing the line in 10.49 sec at the University Stadium in Indianapolis. The flamboyantly styled sprinter, known as "Flo-Jo", was clad in a one-legged purple running suit with turquoise bikini bottoms. She recorded the then second- and third-fastest 100 m times ever at the same trials.

Top 5 fastest women's 100 m

ATHLETE	TIME	LOCATION	DATE
Florence Griffith-Joyner (USA)	10.49 sec	Indianapolis, USA	16 Jul 1988
Elaine Thompson-Herah (JAM)	10.54 sec	Eugene, USA	21 Aug 2021
Shelly-Ann Fraser-Pryce (JAM)	10.60 sec	Lausanne, Switzerland	26 Aug 2021
Florence Griffith-Joyner	10.61 sec	Indianapolis, USA	17 Jul 1988
Elaine Thompson-Herah	10.61 sec	Tokyo, Japan	31 Jul 2021

17 JULY

Golfer Henrik Stenson (SWE) shot a final-round 63 to record the **lowest total score at The Open Championship** in 2016, playing 72 holes at Royal Troon in 264 strokes (68–65–68–63) – 20 under par. Stenson sank 10 birdies in his final round to see off the challenge of Phil Mickelson, in an epic battle dubbed "High Noon at Royal Troon". Stenson became the first Swede to lift the Claret Jug.

18 JULY

At the 2021 Nagoya *basho*, sumo wrestler Hakuhō Shō (JPN) won his final tournament in style, emerging victorious from all 15 of his bouts. It was a record-extending 45th tournament victory in the *makuuchi*, sumo's top division, for the Mongolian-born grappler (b. Mönkhbatyn Davaajargal). Hakuhō retired from the sport with a host of records, including the **most sumo match wins**: 1,187.

Hakuhō's championship wins

TOURNAMENT	MONTH	LOCATION	WINS
Hatsu Basho	January	Tokyo	4
Haru Basho	March	Osaka	9
Natsu Basho	May	Tokyo	8
Nagoya Basho	July	Nagoya	8
Aki Basho	September	Tokyo	7
Kyūshū Basho	November	Fukuoka	9

19 JULY

In 1877, the **first Grand Slam tennis champion** was crowned at the All England Croquet and Lawn Tennis Club in Wimbledon, London, UK. Spencer Gore (UK) defeated William Marshall 6–1, 6–2, 6–4 in 48 min. Gore, who also played first-class cricket for Surrey, is credited with introducing the volley shot to tennis.

20 JULY

In 2006, a modified BAR Honda achieved the **Formula One land-speed record (FIA-approved)**, hitting 397.483 km/h (246.984 mph) over a flying kilometre at Bonneville Salt Flats in the US state of Utah. It was part of Honda's "Bonneville 400" project, to see if an F1 car could reach 400 km/h (248 mph). The supercharged race car was driven by test driver Alan van der Merwe (ZAF), who would later become F1's medical-car driver.

21 JULY

Faith Kipyegon (KEN) ran the **fastest women's one mile** in 4 min 7.64 sec at the 2023 Diamond League meeting in Monaco. She demolished Sifan Hassan's previous mark by almost five seconds. It was Kipyegon's third world record over different distances in just 49 days, following similar unprecedented performances at 1,500 m and 5,000 m.

22 JULY

In 2010, Sri Lankan spinner Muttiah Muralitharan took his 800th Test wicket with his final delivery in his 133rd and final match. He removed tailender Pragyan Ojha on the way to a 10-wicket victory over India. Muralitharan's record for the **most Test match wickets** is almost 100 more than his nearest rival, Australia's Shane Warne (708).

23 JULY

Sarah Sjöström (SWE) swam the **fastest women's 100 m freestyle** in 51.71 sec at the 2017 FINA World Championships in Budapest, Hungary. She set the mark during the first leg of the women's 4 x 100 m freestyle relay final, in which Sweden finished fifth. Sjöström broke the 50 m freestyle world record six days later.

Sarah Sjöström set her first world record – in the 100 m butterfly – in 2009, at the age of 15. Fourteen years later, she broke her own record in the 50 m freestyle at the 2023 World Aquatics Championships. This is the longest gap between individual world records by any swimmer.

24 JULY

In 2015, Ashprihanal Aalto (FIN) achieved the **fastest completion of the Sri Chinmoy Self-Transcendence 3100 Mile Race**, crossing the finish line after 40 days 9 hr 6 min 21 sec. This unusual ultrarunning challenge – equivalent to 119 marathons – is held annually around an extended block in New York City, where conditions often include stifling humidity and downpours of rain. Competitors have 52 days to cover 3,100 mi (4,988 km) – an average of 60 mi (96 km) a day.

25 JULY

Gymnast Oksana Chusovitina (UZB, b. 19 Jun 1975) made history at the Tokyo Olympics in 2021 when she competed in her eighth Games at the age of 46 years 36 days. The **oldest women's Olympic gymnast** finished 14th in qualifying for the vault. Chusovitina had made her Olympic debut back in 1992 – an astonishing 29 years earlier – winning a gold medal in the team all-around competition, representing the Unified Team.

Most women's Olympic appearances

ATHLETE	GAMES	SPAN	SPORT
Nino Salukvadze (Soviet Union, Unified Team, GEO)	10	1988–2024	Shooting
Josefa Idem Guerrini (West Germany, ITA)	8	1984–2012	Canoeing
Lesley Thompson (CAN)	8	1984–2000, 2008–16	Rowing
Oksana Chusovitina (Unified Team, UZB and DEU)	8	1992–2020*	Gymnastics
Claudia Pechstein (DEU)	8	1992–2006**, 2014–22**	Speed skating
Jaqueline Mourão (BRA)	8	2004–08, 2020 2006–22**	Biathlon, cross-country skiing, cycling mountain bike

**Games delayed until 2021* ***Winter Olympics*

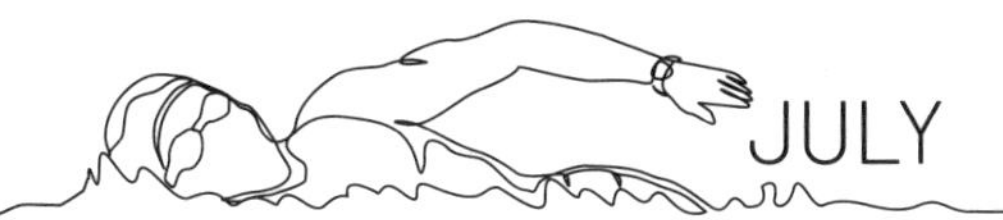

26 JULY

Swimmer Paul Biedermann (DEU) clocked the **fastest men's 400 m freestyle** at the 2009 FINA World Championships in Rome, touching home in 3 min 40.07 sec. The championships took place during the so-called "super-suit" era, when competitors were allowed to wear non-textile swimsuits. A total of 43 world records were broken in eight days.

27 JULY

At the delayed Tokyo Olympics in 2021, Flora Duffy (BMU) won the women's triathlon at Odaiba Marine Park. This made her home nation of Bermuda the **smallest country by population to win an Olympic gold medal**. The North Atlantic archipelago had a population of 62,278 – almost 30,000 less than the capacity of Wembley Stadium.

San Marino is the **smallest country by population to win an Olympic medal** of any colour. The European microstate, with a population of 34,009, claimed a silver in shooting and two bronze (in shooting and wrestling) at the Tokyo Games.

28 JULY

Eric Murray and Hamish Bond (both NZ) produced the **fastest 2,000 m men's coxless pairs row** – 6 min 8.5 sec – during the heats at the 2012 Olympics in London. They smashed the decade-old world-best time by almost six seconds. Murray and Bond were one of the most dominant crews in rowing, winning 69 consecutive races in the men's coxless pairs between 2009 and 2016.

29 JULY

In 2023, Terence Crawford (USA) became the **first four-belt undisputed men's world boxing champion at two weights**. He secured a ninth-round TKO over Errol Spence Jr in Las Vegas to unify the WBA, WBC, WBO and IBF welterweight belts – having previously achieved the same feat at light welterweight in 2017. Crawford's win over Spence was his 40th from 40 professional fights, with 31 KOs.

Four belts at two weights

BOXER	WEIGHTS	DATE
Claressa Shields (USA)	Middleweight, light middleweight	5 Mar 2021
Terence Crawford (USA)	Light welterweight, welterweight	29 Jul 2023
Katie Taylor (IRL)	Lightweight, light welterweight	25 Nov 2023
Naoya Inoue (JPN)	Bantamweight, super bantamweight	26 Dec 2023
Oleksandr Usyk (UKR)	Cruiserweight, heavyweight	18 May 2024

30 JULY

In 2000, Sajjida Shah (PAK, b. 3 Feb 1988) made her Test cricket debut at the age of just 12 years 178 days. The **youngest women's Test cricket player** endured a challenging introduction to the format, contributing just two runs as Pakistan lost to Ireland inside two days at College Park in Dublin. It was the first-ever Test match to be played on Irish soil.

31 JULY

At the 2016 Rally Finland, Kris Meeke (UK) clocked the **fastest average speed at a World Rally Championship event** – 126.62 km/h (78.67 mph). Eight of the 10 fastest WRC rallies have been recorded at the "Grand Prix on Gravel", in the forests around Jyväskylä. The course is renowned for its big jumps and blisteringly fast roads.

1 AUGUST

In 2020, Arsenal defeated Chelsea 2–1 in the FA Cup final, which was delayed from its usual May date and held behind closed doors at Wembley on account of the COVID-19 pandemic. It was the Gunners' 14th victory in the world's oldest existing football competition, which was first held in 1871/72. This is the **most wins of the FA Cup**.

Seven of Arsenal's FA Cup triumphs came under Arsène Wenger between 1998 and 2017 – a record for a manager. Wenger's victory in 2017 – also a 2–1 defeat of Chelsea – broke a tie with George Ramsay, who guided Aston Villa to six FA Cups from 1887 to 1920.

2 AUGUST

At the London 2012 Olympics, the USA racked up the **highest score by a team in a men's Olympic basketball match**, raining down 156 points on Nigeria. The Americans – whose roster was packed with NBA stars such as LeBron James, Kobe Bryant and Kevin Durant – won the game at the North Greenwich Arena by an 83-point margin. Carmelo Anthony scored 37 points in 14 min on court, sinking 10 three-pointers.

3 AUGUST

In 2017, Neymar (BRA) moved to Paris Saint-Germain from Barcelona for a stratospheric €222 m (£198.7 m; $262.8 m) – the **most expensive football transfer**. It more than doubled the previous record of €105 m, which Manchester United paid Juventus for French midfielder Paul Pogba in 2016.

4 AUGUST

MMA star Henry Cejudo (USA) became the **first athlete to win an Olympic and UFC world title** in 2018. A gold medallist from the 2008 Beijing Olympics in freestyle wrestling, Cejudo defeated Demetrious Johnson by split decision at UFC 227 to claim the UFC Flyweight Championship. The following year, Cejudo added the bantamweight title, becoming only the fourth two-weight simultaneous champion in UFC history.

5 AUGUST

At 2007's X Games Los Angeles, John Buffum (USA, b. 4 Oct 1943) took to the start line of the Rally Car Racing event aged 63 years 305 days – making him the **oldest X Games competitor**. Buffum is the USA's most successful rally driver, having won 117 national championship events.

6 AUGUST

Race walker Jesús Ángel García (ESP) achieved the **most Olympic athletics appearances** when he took part in his eighth Games in 2021. García – who made his Olympic debut 29 years earlier, in 1992 – finished 35th in the men's 50 km race walk at Sapporo's Odori Park. He was 51 years old.

7 AUGUST

Jim Furyk (USA) made golfing history in 2016, shooting the **lowest round on the PGA Tour** at the Travelers Championship in Cromwell, Connecticut, USA. He completed 18 holes in just 58 strokes, sinking 10 birdies and an eagle for a round of −12. It was the lowest round of an estimated 1.5 million to have been completed on the PGA Tour at that point.

Furyk's fabulous 58

HOLE	1	2	3	4	5	6	7	8	9	FRONT
SHOTS	4	③	◎2	③	3	④	③	②	③	27
SCORE	E	−1	−3	−4	−4	−5	−6	−7	−8	−8

HOLE	10	11	12	13	14	15	16	17	18	BACK
SHOTS	③	②	③	5	4	4	②	4	4	31
SCORE	−9	−10	−11	−11	−11	−11	−12	−12	−12	−4

8 AUGUST

In 2021, Jason Kenny (UK) claimed the outright record for the **most Olympic track cycling gold medals** – seven – with victory in the men's keirin at the Izu Velodrome in Shizuoka, Japan. He moved one clear of his former teammate, Chris Hoy. Kenny's Olympic titles comprised three in the team sprint, two in the individual sprint and two in the keirin.

9 AUGUST

At the 2012 London Olympics, the "greatest 800 m race ever" was won in extraordinary fashion by Kenya's David Rudisha. The Maasai warrior led from gun to tape to claim both the gold medal and the **fastest men's 800 m** record in 1 min 40.91 sec. All eight runners in the 800 m final ran the fastest-ever Olympic times for their respective finishing positions. Rudisha still owns the fastest three times ever recorded over the distance, and to date is the only athlete to have run under 1 min 41 sec.

10 AUGUST

In 2019, Thailand's women defeated the Netherlands by eight wickets to record the **most consecutive Twenty20 International wins** – 17 matches in a row. Captained by all-rounder Sornnarin Tippoch, Thailand overcame a diverse list of opponents including Myanmar, Kuwait and Scotland.

11 AUGUST

In 2010, David Small (UK) achieved the **longest men's barefoot waterskiing jump** – 29.9 m (98 ft 1 in) – approximately the same length as three London buses. Small, a 19-time IWWF World Open Championship title-winner, was competing at the IWWF World Barefoot Championships in Brandenburg, Germany.

12 AUGUST

At the 1936 Berlin Olympics, diver Marjorie Gestring (USA, b. 18 Nov 1922) became the **youngest Olympic individual gold medallist** at the age of just 13 years 268 days. She won the women's 3 m springboard with her final dive of the competition. Gestring's Olympic career was interrupted by World War II; she almost qualified for the 1948 Games, finishing fourth in the US trials.

13 AUGUST

In 2017, New Zealand scored the **most tries in a Women's Rugby World Cup match** – 19 – during a 121–0 hammering of Hong Kong in Dublin, Ireland. Winger Portia Woodman helped herself to eight. Impressively, this is not even the Black Ferns' biggest World Cup victory: in 1998, they dismantled Germany 134–6.

14 AUGUST

At the fifth Test of the 1948 Ashes cricket series at The Oval in London, Australia's Don Bradman was bowled for a duck in his final Test innings by England spinner Eric Hollies. Bradman, who required only four runs to finish his international career with a batting average of 100, was left on 99.94. This remains the **highest batting average in a men's Test match career** by a distance.

> *"I didn't know it at the time and I don't think the Englishmen knew it either. I think if they had known it they may have been generous enough to let me get four."*
>
> (Don Bradman)

15 AUGUST

At the 1976 Austrian Grand Prix, Maria "Lella" Lombardi (ITA) completed her final drive in F1, finishing in 12th place for Brabham-Ford. She had made the **most Formula One Grand Prix starts by a woman**: 12. Lombardi is one of just two women (along with Maria Teresa de Filippis) to make the start line of an F1 race – and the only one to have scored points, which she achieved at the 1975 Spanish Grand Prix.

16 AUGUST

At the 2009 World Athletics Championships, Usain Bolt (JAM) ran the **fastest men's 100 m** in history, winning the final in 9.58 sec. He shattered his own world record, which he had set exactly a year earlier at the Beijing Olympics. Between 60 m and 80 m, Bolt reached a top speed of 44.72 km/h (27.78 mph), covering 20 m in just 1.61 sec.

> **The greatest sprinter in the history of athletics, Usain Bolt won the 100 m and 200 m at three consecutive Olympics between 2008 and 2016. He still holds the world records for the 200 m – 19.19 sec – and the 4 x 100 m relay – 36.84 sec (together with teammates Nesta Carter, Michael Frater and Yohan Blake).**

17 AUGUST

Swimmer Michael Phelps (USA) secured his eighth gold medal at the 2008 Beijing Olympics with victory in the men's 4 x 100 m medley relay. It completed one of the great sporting feats – the **most gold medals at a single Olympic Games**. Phelps broke world records in seven of the eight events. His time in the 400 m individual medley stood for 15 years, until it was finally broken by France's Léon Marchand at the 2023 World Aquatics Championships.

Phelps's Golden Games

EVENT	DATE	TIME	RECORD
400 m medley	10 Aug	4 min 3.84 sec	World
4 x 100 m freestyle	11 Aug	3 min 8.24 sec	World
200 m freestyle	12 Aug	1 min 42.96 sec	World
200 m butterfly	13 Aug	1 min 52.03 sec	World
4 x 200 m freestyle	13 Aug	6 min 58.56 sec	World
200 m medley	15 Aug	1 min 54.23 sec	World
100 m butterfly	16 Aug	50.58 sec	Olympic
4 x 100 m medley	17 Aug	3 min 29.34 sec	World

18 AUGUST

At the 2018 Rugby Championship, New Zealand lock Sam Whitelock played in his 100th international, a 38–13 win over Australia. Just 8 years 67 days had elapsed since his debut for the All Blacks – the **fastest time to win 100 international rugby union caps**. Whitelock lost only eight of those games, fewer than any other centurion.

19 AUGUST

Mark Vetter (USA) racked up the **highest tenpin bowling score between the legs** – 280 out of 300 – at The Back Bowl in Eagle, Colorado, USA, in 2014. He threw 11 strikes and a spare, releasing the ball between his legs each time. "Never underestimate the motivational power of beer," the record holder declared afterwards.

20 AUGUST

In 2022, Harry Kane (UK) notched his 185th league goal for Tottenham Hotspur to claim the record for the **most English Premier League goals for one club**. He had surpassed the mark of Manchester City striker Sergio Agüero. Kane went on to increase his tally to 213 before leaving Spurs for Bayern Munich at the end of the 2022/23 season.

Most EPL goals for one club

PLAYER	TEAM	GOALS
Harry Kane (UK)	Tottenham Hotspur	213
Sergio Agüero (ARG)	Manchester City	184
Wayne Rooney (UK)	Manchester United	183
Mo Salah (EGY)	Liverpool	182
Thierry Henry (FRA)	Arsenal	175

21 AUGUST

The **oldest Olympic athletics gold medallist** was crowned at the 1920 Antwerp Games. Patrick "Babe" McDonald (USA, b. IRL, 29 Jul 1878) won the 56 lb weight throw aged 42 years 23 days. A New York City policeman who regularly patrolled Times Square, McDonald was an imposing figure who stood 6 ft 5 in (1.95 m) tall. The 56 lb weight throw was never held at the Games again, leaving his winning effort of 11.265 m (36 ft 11 in) as the Olympic record to this day.

Pat McDonald was one of a group of North American Olympic throwers in the early 20th century christened the "Irish Whales" by contemporary sportswriters. They earned the nickname on account of their Irish heritage, great size, enormous appetites and prodigious athletic feats. Other "Whales" included discus thrower Martin Sheridan and hammer thrower John Flanagan, both of whom won three Olympic gold medals.

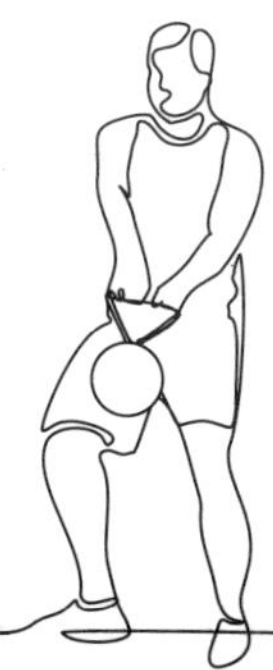

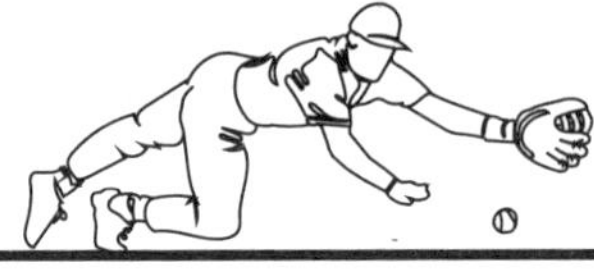

22 AUGUST

In 2007, the Texas Rangers scored the **most runs in an MLB game**, romping to a 30–3 victory over the Baltimore Orioles at Camden Yards in Maryland. This is a modern-era record (i.e., post-1900). The Rangers actually trailed 3–0 after the first three innings – they went on to score five runs in the fourth inning, nine in the sixth, 10 in the eighth and another six in the ninth.

23 AUGUST

Ashrita Furman (USA) completed the **fastest 10-km sack race** in 2001, bouncing around a course in Montauk, on New York's Long Island, in 1 hr 22 min 2 sec. A serial record breaker, Furman claimed his first GWR record title in 1979 by completing 27,000 jumping jacks (star jumps). He has since gone on to break more than 600 world records.

24 AUGUST

In 2014, Kirsty Johnson (UK) plunged her way to the **fastest women's time at the World Bog Snorkelling Championships** – 1 min 22.56 sec. Competitors at the annual event in the Welsh town of Llanwrtyd Wells must complete two lengths of a murky 55-m-long (180-ft) trench. Snorkels, masks and flippers are required; fancy dress is optional.

25 AUGUST

Emma Raducanu (UK, b. CAN) began her qualifying campaign for the 2021 US Open with a 61-min dismissal of Bibiane Schoofs. It was the beginning of one of tennis's greatest triumphs, as Raducanu marched through three qualifying and seven main-draw matches to win the title – without dropping a set. Ranked 150 in the world, and playing in only her fourth WTA event, she became the **first qualifier to win an open-era Grand Slam singles title**.

Raducanu's "Fairytale of New York"

ROUND	OPPONENT	SCORE
First qualifying	Bibiane Schoofs (NLD)	6–1, 6–2
Second qualifying	Mariam Bolkvadze (GEO)	6–3 , 7–5
Third qualifying	Mayar Sherif (EGY)	6–1, 6–4
First round	Stefanie Vögele (CHE)	6–2, 6–3
Second round	Zhang Shuai (CHN)	6–2, 6–4
Third round	Sara Sorribes Tormo (ESP)	6–0, 6–1
Fourth round	Shelby Rogers (USA)	6–2, 6–1
Quarter-final	Belinda Bencic (CHE)	6–3, 6–4
Semi-final	Maria Sakkari (GRC)	6–1, 6–4
Final	Leylah Fernandez (CAN)	6–4, 6–3

26 AUGUST

Golfer Lydia Ko (NZ, b. KOR, 24 Apr 1997) won the CN Canadian Women's Open in 2012 to become the **youngest winner on the LPGA Tour**, aged 15 years 124 days old. Ko finished on -13, three shots clear of second place at Vancouver Golf Club.

Ko was unable to claim the $300,000 (£187,700) first prize on account of her amateur status. But she soon made up for it. Upon turning professional in 2013, it took Ko just 16 events on the LPGA Tour to earn $1 m in prize money – and all before her 18th birthday.

27 AUGUST

In 2017, Tomokazu Harimoto (JPN, b. CHN, Zhang Zhihe, 27 Jun 2003) stunned the table tennis world by winning the Czech Open at the age of 14 years 61 days. He defeated Olympic champions Ma Long and Zhang Jike en route to the title. Harimoto remains the **youngest winner of an International Table Tennis Federation World Tour men's singles title**.

28 AUGUST

During a second-round qualifier for the 1983 US Open, Barbara "Barbie" Bramblett (USA) found herself trailing 0–6, 0–5 against Ann Hulbert and facing three match points at love–40. Remarkably, the 18-year-old Bramblett rallied to win the match 0–6, 7–5, 6–3, saving 18 match points in the process. This is the **greatest comeback in a women's professional tennis match**.

> *"I started swinging out on the ball, and my game elevated miraculously. It was a literal miracle. Every ball I hit skidded on the line."*
>
> (Barbie Bramblett)

29 AUGUST

The 2015 Challenge Cup final saw rugby league's Leeds Rhinos stomp Hull Kingston Rovers by a record-breaking score of 50–0 at Wembley Stadium in London. Winger Tom Briscoe helped himself to the **most tries in a Challenge Cup final**, touching down five times.

30 AUGUST

The 1992 Belgian Grand Prix was won by Benetton's 23-year-old driver Michael Schumacher (DEU), who also recorded the fastest lap of the race. It was the first of 77 superlative circuits that Schumacher went on to complete over the course of his career – the **most Formula One fastest laps**.

> **To date, a total of 139 drivers have set the fastest lap of a Formula One race. The first was Giuseppe "Nino" Farina, driving for Alfa Romeo at the 1950 British Grand Prix; the most recent was Alpine's Esteban Ocon, at the 2024 US Grand Prix.**

31 AUGUST

In the final of the 2008 AVP Crocs Cup Shootout beach volleyball tournament, the pairing of Misty May-Treanor and Kerri Walsh Jennings (both USA) lost to Elaine Youngs and Nicole Branagh in a gruelling encounter that finished 21–19, 10–21, 25–23 and lasted 1 hr 45 min – the second-longest women's volleyball match in AVP history. It was the first time that May-Treanor and Walsh Jennings had tasted defeat in more than a year. In that time they had claimed 19 titles and amassed the **most consecutive beach volleyball wins by a women's team** – 112.

1 SEPTEMBER

At her final tennis tournament, the 2022 US Open, Serena Williams defeated world No.2 Anett Kontaveit in the second round to extend her record for the **most Grand Slam women's singles match wins** to 367. Williams lost in the third round as the curtain came down on a glittering career that had seen her become a 23-time Grand Slam singles champion.

> **Serena Williams won her first Grand Slam singles match at the 1998 Australian Open, defeating Irina Spîrlea 6–7, 6–3, 6–1 at the age of just 16. She was knocked out in the second round by her elder sister, Venus. The Williams sisters went on to face each other in nine Grand Slam finals, with Serena emerging victorious on seven occasions.**

2 SEPTEMBER

Courtney Dauwalter (USA) crossed the finish line of the 2023 Ultra-Trail du Mont-Blanc to complete the **first ultrarunning "Triple Crown"**. Following on from her victories at the Western States 100 and the Hardrock 100, Dauwalter had won three prestigious 100-mi (161-km) races in just 10 weeks. She covered 310.7 mi (500 km) and 25,500 m (83,660 ft) of elevation gain – almost the same as climbing Everest from sea level 10 times.

3 SEPTEMBER

In 2021, Diede de Groot (NLD) won Paralympic gold to complete the **first Career Golden Slam in wheelchair tennis singles**. She had completed her full set of four Grand Slam tournament titles – Wimbledon and the Australian, French and US Opens – in 2019. De Groot added the Paralympic title with a 6–3, 7–6 win over Yui Kamiji at Ariake Tennis Park.

4 SEPTEMBER

In 2020, Mo Farah (UK, b. SOM, Hussein Abdi Kahin) broke athletics' **men's one hour** record, running 21.33 km (13.25 mi) in 60 min at the King Baudouin Stadium in Brussels, Belgium. He broke Haile Gebrselassie's previous mark by 45 m to claim his first track world record at the age of 37.

> *"It isn't supposed to be easy to break a world record, but I can tell you that was really hard."*
>
> (Mo Farah)

5 SEPTEMBER

During qualifying for the 2020 Italian Grand Prix, Mercedes driver Lewis Hamilton (UK) completed a lap of the 5.7-km-long (3.5-mi) Monza circuit in 1 min 18.887 sec. This is the **highest average lap speed at a Formula One Grand Prix** – 264.362 km/h (164.267 mph).

Known as the "Temple of Speed", the Autodromo Nazionale di Monza is famed for its long straights and fast corners. Ferrari's Michael Schumacher won the 2003 Italian Grand Prix averaging a speed of 247.585 km/h (153.842 mph) over 53 laps – the **highest average race speed at a Formula One Grand Prix**.

6 SEPTEMBER

In 2016, Guatemala thumped St Vincent and the Grenadines 9–3 in a FIFA World Cup qualifying match. Striker Carlos Ruiz scored five times in his final international to take his record for the **most goals in FIFA World Cup qualifiers** to 39. To date, Ruiz stands three clear of Portugal's Cristiano Ronaldo.

7 SEPTEMBER

Aries Merritt (USA) ran the **fastest men's 110 m hurdles** in 12.80 sec at a 2012 Diamond League meeting in Brussels, Belgium. He added the world record to the gold medal he had won at the London Olympics the previous month.

The first world record holder in the 110 m hurdles was US athlete Forrest Smithson, who set a time of 15 sec at the 1908 London Olympics. A divinity student and devout Christian, Smithson was said to have won Olympic gold while carrying a Bible in one hand – a popular myth, owing to a photo he posed for while out of competition.

8 SEPTEMBER

Italy beat Lithuania 5–0 in 2021 to stretch their record for the **longest unbeaten run in men's international football** to 37 matches. The *Azzurri* won 28 and drew nine games during their three-year run – scoring 93 goals and conceding 12 – and winning the delayed UEFA Euro 2020 tournament. Italy's unbeaten streak ended with a 2–1 defeat to Spain in the UEFA Nations League on 6 Oct 2021.

9 SEPTEMBER

In 2007, Roger Federer (CHE) secured his fourth successive US Open title with a straight-sets win over Novak Djokovic. The Swiss ace also set a record for the **most consecutive men's Grand Slam singles finals**, having reached 10 in a row across a three-year span. Remarkably, Federer won eight of his 10 finals, losing out only at the 2006 and 2007 French Opens to his great rival, Rafael Nadal.

10 SEPTEMBER

In 2016, Brent Harvey (AUS) made his 432nd and final appearance for North Melbourne – the **most Australian rules football games played**. An AFL premiership winner in 1999 and a four-time All-Australian, "Boomer" is one of only six players – along with Dustin Fletcher, Scott Pendlebury, Kevin Bartlett, Shaun Burgoyne and Michael Tuck – to make 400 career appearances.

11 SEPTEMBER

West Ham United scored a late consolation during their 3–1 defeat to Chelsea in 2010 to end a remarkable run by their West London opponents. Chelsea had racked up the **most unanswered English Premier League goals**, scoring 35 times without reply. Their run stretched eight games across two seasons and included 8–0 and 6–0 humblings of the same opponent – the unfortunate Wigan Athletic.

12 SEPTEMBER

Natalie du Toit (ZAF) swam the **fastest women's 400 m freestyle (S9)** – 4 min 23.81 sec – at the 2008 Paralympic Games in Beijing, China. Du Toit, who became a below-the-knee amputee at the age of 17 following a scooter accident, also competed at the 2008 Olympics, finishing 16th in the 10 km open-water swimming event.

> *"I always had a dream to take part in an Olympic Games, and losing my leg didn't change anything."*
>
> (Natalie du Toit)

13 SEPTEMBER

The **first New York City Marathon** took place in 1970. A total of 126 men and one woman started the race in Central Park, with 55 crossing the finish line. The winner was the USA's Gary Muhrcke, in 2 hr 31 min 38 sec. Muhrcke, a firefighter, nearly didn't enter the race as he had been up all night tackling blazes. He received a wristwatch and a recycled sports trophy for his efforts.

Gary Muhrcke went on to win the first-ever Empire State Building Run-Up in 1978. He climbed 86 flights and 1,576 steps to reach the top of the famous New York landmark in 12 min 33 sec.

14 SEPTEMBER

At the 2022 US International Classic in Lake Placid, New York, figure skater Ilia Malinin (USA) performed the **first quadruple Axel in competition**. The only jump with a forward take-off – meaning that it comprises an extra half-revolution – the Axel was the last to be successfully executed as a quadruple. Malinin, aka the "Quad God", would go on to become the first skater to attempt quads in all six jumps (toe loop, Salchow, loop, flip, Lutz and Axel) in a single programme.

15 SEPTEMBER

Rhyne Howard (USA) recorded the **most points in a debut WNBA postseason game** in 2023, scoring 36 points for the Atlanta Dream in a 94–82 loss against the Dallas Wings. The No.1 draft pick and 2022 Rookie of the Year dropped 19 of those in the first quarter, the most in league history in the opening period.

16 SEPTEMBER

Kevin Mayer (FRA) scored the **most points in a men's decathlon** – 9,126 – at the 2018 Décastar Combined Events Challenge in Talence, France. His effort included a high jump competition involving an energy-sapping 12 jumps, which he described as "apocalyptic". Coincidentally, Mayer scored exactly the same number of points on both days of competition: 4,563.

Mayer's Magnificent 10

EVENT	MEASUREMENT	EVENT	MEASUREMENT
100 m	10.55 sec	Long jump	7.80 m
Shot put	16.00 m	High jump	2.05 m
400 m	48.42 sec	110 m hurdles	13.75 sec
Discus throw	50.54 m	Pole vault	5.45 m
Javelin throw	71.90 m	1500 m	4 min 36.11 sec

17 SEPTEMBER

Bayern Munich (DEU) scored the **most goals by a team in a UEFA Champions League match** in 2024, thumping Dinamo Zagreb 9–2 at the Allianz Arena. Bayern's English striker Harry Kane became the first player to successfully convert three penalties in a single game in the competition.

18 SEPTEMBER

At the 2016 Paralympics in Rio de Janeiro, Brazil, Iran claimed their sixth men's sitting volleyball title, defeating Bosnia and Herzegovina in the gold-medal match by 3 sets to 1. Their players included Morteza Mehrzad Selakjani, who at 2.46 m (8 ft 0.85 in) is not only the **tallest Paralympian**, but the third-tallest living person.

Morteza Mehrzad Selakjani won his third consecutive Olympic gold medal at the Paris Games in 2024. In the final against Bosnia and Herzegovina, he top-scored with 27 points.

19 SEPTEMBER

In 1998, Cal Ripken Jr (USA) played his 2,632nd game in a row for the Baltimore Orioles – the **most consecutive MLB games**. The "Iron Man" hadn't missed a match since 30 May 1982, passing Lou Gehrig's mark of 2,130 games in 1995. Ripken Jr took himself out of the Orioles' line-up against the New York Yankees the next day, bringing the curtain down on one of baseball's most enduring records.

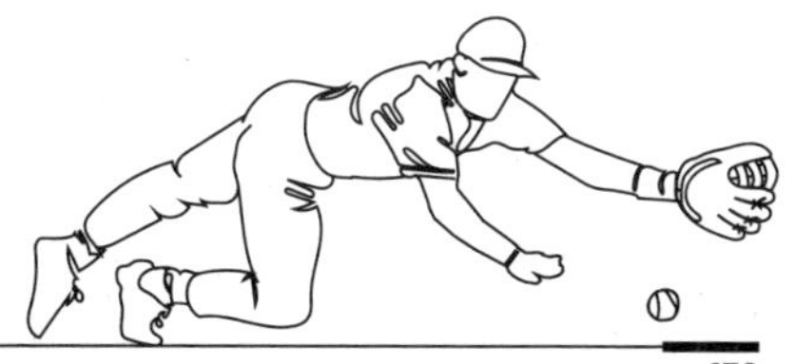

20 SEPTEMBER

The **youngest judo world champion** was crowned in 2018, when Daria Bilodid (UKR, b. 10 Oct 2000) claimed the women's -48 kg title in Baku, Azerbaijan, aged 17 years 345 days. Bilodid – nicknamed the "Anaconda" on account of her ground skills – took up the combat sport at the age of six, having switched from gymnastics.

21 SEPTEMBER

At the 1904 Games in St Louis, Missouri, USA, Eliza Pollock (USA, b. 24 Oct 1840) became the **oldest Olympic women's gold medallist** at the age of 63 years 333 days. She was a member of the Cincinnati Archers team who won the archery women's team round – the only team to enter the event.

22 SEPTEMBER

In 2020, freestyler Maya Fung (USA) achieved the **most football touches in one hour**, juggling the ball 13,300 times in 60 min in Prosper, Texas, USA. She had practised for three years for the record attempt. Despite averaging more than three touches every second, Maya didn't let the ball touch the floor once over the course of the hour. She beat the existing men's record by more than 1,400 touches.

23 SEPTEMBER

Boxer Henry Armstrong (USA) KO'd Phil Furr in the fourth round in 1940 to defend his welterweight world title for the 18th time in less than two years. This is the **most consecutive world welterweight title defences**. "Homicide Hank" had won the belt with a dominant performance against Barney Ross in May 1938.

Armstrong was named 1937's Fighter of the Year by *The Ring* magazine, having compiled an astonishing record of 27 wins – 26 by knockout – and no defeats in the calendar year. In 1938, Armstrong would simultaneously hold the featherweight, welterweight and lightweight world titles. He is the only boxer in history to hold belts at three weights at the same time.

24 SEPTEMBER

In 2010, Cincinnati Reds pitcher Aroldis Chapman (CUB) unleashed the **fastest MLB pitch**, measured at 105.8 mph (170.2 km/h). He was facing Tony Gwynn Jr in the eighth inning of the Reds' game against the San Diego Padres at Petco Park. Chapman, nicknamed the "Cuban Missile", threw eight of the 10 fastest pitches recorded in the Statcast era.

25 SEPTEMBER

In 2016, Castleford Tigers winger Denny Solomona (SAM/UK, b. NZ) went over for a hat-trick of tries as Widnes Vikings were despatched 40–26. It took Solomona's total for the season to 40 – the **most tries in a Super League season**. Born in New Zealand, he played international rugby league for Samoa and went on to represent England in rugby union.

26 SEPTEMBER

Welsh winger George North (b. 13 Apr 1992) became the **youngest Rugby World Cup try scorer** at the 2011 tournament in New Zealand. North was 19 years 166 days old when he dotted down during Wales's 81–7 thrashing of Namibia at Stadium Taranaki in New Plymouth.

George North retired from international rugby in 2024. His total of 49 tries (47 for Wales, two for the British & Irish Lions) placed him joint-seventh on the all-time men's list. Top of the table is Japan's Daisuke Ohata, who scored 69 tries between 1996 and 2006.

27 SEPTEMBER

During a One-Day International against England in 2017, the West Indies' Evin Lewis (TTO) made the **highest score by a batter retired hurt**. He hit 176 runs before inside-edging a ball into his foot, leaving him unable to continue. The previous all-format record of 165 had been set by Australia's Charles Bannerman during the first-ever Test match in 1877.

> **Sri Lankan batter Roshan Mahanama retired hurt seven times in international one-day cricket – more than any other player. In 1989, he was forced to leave the field having been struck amidships with consecutive deliveries by pace bowler Wasim Akram. A member of Sri Lanka's 1996 Cricket World Cup-winning side, Mahanama later fell out of favour with the selectors and referenced his dissatisfaction over the ending of his international career in his autobiography, entitled *Retired Hurt*.**

28 SEPTEMBER

Quarterback Patrick Mahomes (USA) reached 10,000 career passing yards during the Kansas City Chiefs' 34–20 victory over the Baltimore Ravens in 2020. It was only Mahomes's 34th game in the NFL – the **fewest games to reach 10,000 passing yards**. He bested the previous record by two games.

29 SEPTEMBER

In 2019, João Vieira (PRT, b. 20 Feb 1976) became the **oldest medallist at the World Athletics Championships**, winning silver in the men's 50 km race walk aged 43 years 221 days. The event had begun at 11.30 p.m. the previous evening on account of the heat in Doha, Qatar.

> *"For me, it was hell – very, very hot. How did I cope? A lot of ice and cold water."*
>
> (João Vieira)

30 SEPTEMBER

The first staging of the Gordon Bennett Cup took place in 1906, with aeronauts challenged to fly their gas balloons as far as possible from the launch site in Paris's Tuileries Garden. Sixteen balloons took part; the winning pilots were Lt Frank Lahm and Major Henry Hersey (both USA), who flew 641.10 km (398.36 mi) before landing in the northern English county of Yorkshire. Still flown today, the Gordon Bennett Cup is the **oldest aviation race**.

1 OCTOBER

In 1988, Steffi Graf (DEU) completed the **first tennis Golden Slam**. The 19-year-old defeated Gabriela Sabatini 6–3, 6–3 in the Olympic final, having won all four Grand Slam women's singles titles that year. Graf had been the unofficial defending Olympic champion, having won the tennis demonstration event in Los Angeles in 1984 at the age of 15.

The final of the 1988 French Open saw Graf at her most dominant. She dismantled Natasha Zvereva 6–0, 6–0 in just 34 min – the only time a so-called "double bagel" has been recorded in a Grand Slam final.

2 OCTOBER

The **youngest winner of the World Rally Championship** was crowned in 2022, when Kalle Rovanperä (FIN, b. 1 Oct 2000) triumphed at the Rally New Zealand in Auckland to seal the title a day after his 22nd birthday. Kalle, the son of former WRC driver Harri Rovanperä, won six of 13 rallies that year, alongside co-driver Jonne Halttunen.

3 OCTOBER

In 1992, Maurizio Damilano (ITA) achieved the **fastest men's 30,000 m race walk** – 2 hr 1 min 44 sec – in Cuneo, Italy. Damilano was a two-time world champion in the 20 km walk and claimed the Olympic gold in 1980. His twin brother Giorgio was also a race walker, and they were coached by their elder brother Sandro.

4 OCTOBER

Aged 18 years 318 days, Freddie Lindstrom (USA, b. 21 Nov 1905) became the **youngest player in an MLB World Series** in 1924. He played for the New York Giants against the Washington Senators. Despite contributing 10 hits across the series and a .333 batting average, Lindstrom is perhaps best remembered for the "bad hop" he suffered while fielding during the 12th inning of the deciding Game 7 – the ball took an unexpected bounce and flew over his head, allowing the Senators to score the Series-clinching run.

5 OCTOBER

Rohit Sharma (IND) blasted the **most sixes in a men's Test cricket match** – a total of 13, across two innings – against South Africa in 2019. Sharma hit centuries in both innings, racking up six sixes in his first innings of 176 and seven in his second of 127. The previous record of 12, by Pakistan's Wasim Akram in one innings against Zimbabwe, had stood since 1996.

6 OCTOBER

In 2023, Simone Biles (USA) extended her record for the **most women's all-around titles at the World Artistic Gymnastics Championships** with her sixth victory in the event. The winner of the individual all-around is determined by combining the score of all four apparatus for women – vault, uneven bars, balance beam and floor. Widely regarded as one of the greatest-ever gymnasts, Biles has won a record 30 world championship medals, 23 of them gold.

Biles's World Championship Medals

EVENT	GOLD	SILVER	BRONZE
Team	5		
Individual all-around	6		
Vault	2	3	1
Balance beam	4		2
Floor exercise	6		
Uneven bars		1	
TOTAL	**23**	**4**	**3**

7 OCTOBER

Jockey Frankie Dettori (ITA) won the 2018 Prix de l'Arc de Triomphe, riding Enable to victory for the second successive year. Dettori had previously won Europe's richest horse race on board Lammtarra (1995), Sakhee (2001), Marienbard (2002) and Golden Horn (2015) – the **most Prix de l'Arc de Triomphe wins by a jockey** (6).

8 OCTOBER

Kelvin Kiptum (KEN) ran the **fastest men's marathon** in 2023, winning the Chicago Marathon in 2 hr 35 sec. He broke the previous record by more than 30 sec. Tragically, Kiptum was killed in a car accident on 11 Feb 2024 at the age of 24. He had run just three marathons, achieving the first-, third- and seventh-fastest times ever over the distance.

9 OCTOBER

In the second game of the 1916 World Series, Boston Red Sox pitcher George Herman "Babe" Ruth (USA) completed the **most innings pitched in a World Series game** – 14 – against the Brooklyn Robins. Though Ruth would gain renown as a home-run-hitting slugger, the "Sultan of Swat" started out as a left-handed pitcher. The Red Sox won their marathon tussle with the Robins 2–1, thanks to a pinch-hit single by Del Gainer in the bottom of the 14th.

10 OCTOBER

Michèle Mouton (FRA) made motorsport history at the 1981 Rallye Sanremo in Italy, becoming the first woman to win a World Rally Championship race. She was driving an Audi Quattro alongside co-driver Fabrizia Pons. Mouton claimed three more victories in 1982, narrowly missing out on the championship title. Her total of four is the **most World Rally Championship race wins by a woman**.

> *"When you are in the car, nobody can say [whether] it's a man or a woman driving."*
>
> (Michèle Mouton)

11 OCTOBER

In 2008, Choi Hyun-mi (KOR, b. PRK, 7 Nov 1990) won the vacant WBA women's featherweight title in her first professional bout, against China's Xu Chun Yan. This is the **fewest fights to win a boxing world title**. Choi – who fought under the nickname "Defector Girl Boxer", on account of her family moving from North to South Korea in 2004 – was aged 17 years 339 days, making her also the **youngest women's boxing world champion**.

12 OCTOBER

Wide receiver Randal Williams (USA) scored the **fastest NFL touchdown** in 2003, playing for the Dallas Cowboys against the Philadelphia Eagles. He caught the ball from an attempted onside kick and returned it 37 yards for a TD with just 3 sec taken off the official clock – although an issue with the timing meant that it had not started until at least a couple of seconds after kick-off.

13 OCTOBER

At UFC 153 in 2012, Anderson Silva (BRA) knocked out Stephan Bonnar in Rio de Janeiro to take his record for the **most consecutive UFC fight wins** to 16. The middleweight champion, nicknamed "The Spider", lost his next bout against Chris Weidman at UFC 162 the following year. Silva's streak included 10 defences of his middleweight title, which he held for more than six years.

Longest UFC title reigns

FIGHTER	DIVISION	DEFENCES	REIGN
Anderson Silva (BRA)	Middleweight	10	6 years 267 days
Demetrious Johnson (USA)	Flyweight	11	5 years 317 days
Georges St-Pierre (CAN)	Welterweight	9	5 years 239 days
Amanda Nunes (BRA)	Women's Bantamweight	5	5 years 156 days
José Aldo (BRA)	Featherweight	7	5 years 23 days

14 OCTOBER

In 2023, Lucy Charles-Barclay (UK) claimed her first women's IRONMAN world championship in style at Kailua-Kona in Hawaii. She completed the 2.4-mi swim in 49 min 36 sec, rode 112 mi in 4 hr 32 min 29 sec and then ran a marathon in 2 hr 57 min 38 sec. Her total time, including transitions, was 8 hr 24 min 31 sec – the **fastest women's time at the IRONMAN® World Championship**.

15 OCTOBER

Uruguay's Diego Ormaechea (b. 19 Sep 1959) became the **oldest player to appear in a Rugby Union World Cup match** in 1999. The veteran number eight was aged 40 years 26 days when he took to the field against South Africa at Hampden Park in Glasgow. Ormaechea is also the tournament's **oldest try scorer**, having touched down against Spain 13 days earlier.

16 OCTOBER

At rugby league's Emerging Nations Tournament in 1995, Ireland defeated Moldova 48–26 at Spotland Stadium in Rochdale, UK. The man of the match was the Wolfhounds' full-back Gavin Gordon, who scored a hat-trick of tries. Gordon (b. 28 Feb 1978) was just 17 years 230 days old, making him the **youngest rugby league international**.

17 OCTOBER

Game 6 of the 1978 World Series saw the New York Yankees defeat the LA Dodgers 7–2 to win the championship by four games to two. An average of 44.27 million viewers tuned in to the NBC broadcast for each game – the **largest TV audience for an MLB World Series**.

18 OCTOBER

At the 1968 Olympics in Mexico City, long jumper Bob Beamon (USA) flew out to an astonishing 8.90 m (29 ft 2 in) at the Estadio Olímpico Universitario. He leapt so far that the optical measuring device ran out of rail and a tape measure had to be used to gauge the distance. Beamon's jump was the long jump world record for 23 years, until 1991, and remains the **longest-standing Olympic athletics** record to this day. No one has bettered it at the 14 Games since.

> **Beamon's record-breaking jump nearly didn't happen at all. He fouled twice during qualifying for the 1968 Olympic final and only had one effort left – his teammate Ralph Boston suggested that Beamon take off early, far back from the board. Beamon took his advice, and qualified easily on the third attempt.**

19 OCTOBER

In the semi-final of the 2018 Stihl Timbersports Team World Championship in Liverpool, Australia (Jamie Head, Brayden Meyer, Brad De Losa and Glen Gillam) – aka the "Chopperoos" – completed the **fastest timber sports team relay** in 45.10 sec. The event consists of four elements: the stock saw, underhand chop, single buck and standing block chop.

20 OCTOBER

In 2012, welterweight champion Randall Bailey (USA) lost his IBF world title to Devon Alexander by unanimous decision after a cagey encounter that had fans inside New York City's Barclays Center booing at ringside. CompuBox recorded Bailey landing just 45 blows during the entirety of the contest – the **fewest punches in a 12-round boxing world title fight**. Ironically, Bailey's nickname was "The Knock-Out King", on account of his hard-hitting prowess.

21 OCTOBER

In 1989, Jimmy Connors (USA) won the Tel Aviv Open to claim his 109th and final tennis singles title. The 37-year-old defeated Gilad Bloom 2–6, 6–2, 6–1. Connors still holds the record for the **most men's singles tournament titles**, standing six clear of Roger Federer. Eight of Connors' titles were won at Grand Slams, including five at the US Open.

22 OCTOBER

Marco Hepp (DEU) achieved the **fastest men's speed skydiving (FAI-approved)** in 2022, clocking an average vertical speed of 529.77 km/h (329.18 mph) across a three-second window of freefall. He was competing at the 4th Fédération Aéronautique Internationale World Speed Skydiving Championships in Eloy, Arizona, USA. Hepp set three world records in eight jumps – his slowest was 522.9 km/h (324.9 mph).

> *"I tried hard to do it right – train properly, eat well, sleep well, and don't land on any rattlesnakes in the desert."*
>
> (Marco Hepp)

23 OCTOBER

Manchester City routed Sparta Prague 5–0 in 2024 to claim the record for the **longest unbeaten run in the UEFA Champions League** – 26 games – from their local rivals, Manchester United. City's streak began on 6 Sep 2022 and comprised 18 wins and eight draws. They won the 2022/23 Champions League and exited the competition the next year on penalties, after two draws against Real Madrid.

24 OCTOBER

In 2010, Matteo Manassero (ITA, b. 19 Apr 1993) became the **youngest winner on the DP World Tour** – then called the PGA European Tour – when he won the Castelló Masters Costa Azahar in Spain aged 17 years 188 days. Manassero finished on -16, four shots clear of his nearest rival. The Italian putting prodigy had already claimed The Amateur Championship the previous year.

> **In 2020, Matteo Manassero stepped away from golf after sinking to 1,805th on the Official World Golf Ranking. But he rebuilt his game and made a triumphant comeback on the DP World Tour, winning the Jonsson Workwear Open in South Africa on 10 Mar 2024 – more than a decade after his last victory.**

25 OCTOBER

At the 2003 Rugby World Cup, hosts Australia inflicted a 142–0 whipping on Namibia in Adelaide. The Wallabies ran in a record 22 tries, with Chris Latham helping himself to five, while Mat Rogers scored 42 points (two tries and 16 conversions). This is the **largest margin of victory in a Rugby World Cup match**.

> **Minnows Namibia were largely comprised of amateur players. Their squad for the 2003 Rugby World Cup contained Rudie van Vuuren, who had also represented Namibia at the Cricket World Cup earlier that same year.**

26 OCTOBER

At UFC Fight Night 30 in 2013, women's bantamweight Jéssica Andrade (BRA) achieved her first win in the Octagon, earning a unanimous decision over Rosi Sexton. Andrade would go on to rack up the **most UFC women's wins** – surpassing Amanda Nunes with her 17th victory, achieved at UFC 300 on 13 Apr 2024.

27 OCTOBER

Terrelle Pryor (USA) of the Oakland Raiders scored the **longest touchdown run by an NFL quarterback** – 93 yards – against the Pittsburgh Steelers in 2013. Pryor made history on the first play of the game from scrimmage.

28 OCTOBER

At the 1904 Olympic Games in St Louis, Missouri, USA, gymnast George Eyser (USA, b. DEU) won six medals in a day, including golds in rope climbing, parallel bars and the vault. His feat was all the more amazing for the fact that he competed with a prosthetic wooden leg; he lost his left leg in his youth after being run over by a train. Eyser was the **first amputee to compete at an Olympic Games**.

29 OCTOBER

During the Golden State Warriors' 149–124 victory over the Chicago Bulls in 2018, guard Klay Thompson (USA) sank the **most three-point field goals in an NBA game** – 14. He finished the game with 52 points in just under 27 min of play. Thompson took the three-point record from Stephen Curry, his teammate and fellow "Splash Brother".

30 OCTOBER

In 1974, George Foreman (USA) lost his heavyweight world championship to Muhammad Ali in "The Rumble in the Jungle" in Kinshasa, Zaire (now the Democratic Republic of the Congo). The fearsome Foreman was the heavy pre-fight favourite, but Ali adopted a "rope-a-dope" strategy to wear Foreman down before delivering a knockout blow in the eighth round. Foreman had to wait 20 years 7 days to become heavyweight champion again: on 5 Nov 1994, he knocked out Michael Moorer to claim the WBA and IBF belts. This is the **longest time between boxing world heavyweight titles**.

31 OCTOBER

New Zealand won the Rugby World Cup final in 2015, beating their Antipodean rivals Australia 34–17 at London's Twickenham Stadium. All Black fly-half Dan Carter closed out his international career with a man-of-the-match performance, kicking 19 points. He retired having scored the **most rugby union international points** – 1,598.

Carter's last kick in international rugby was a conversion of Beauden Barrett's 79th-min try. He took it with his right foot – the only one of his 293 successful conversions Carter didn't strike with his left.

1 NOVEMBER

The Houston Astros won Game 7 of the 2017 MLB World Series to claim the championship over the Los Angeles Dodgers. Astros slugger George Springer hit his fifth home run of the series, equalling the feat of Reggie Jackson and Chase Utley (all USA). Springer's dingers accounted for 20 of the 29 bases he made across the seven games – the **most total bases in a World Series**.

> Total bases is a baseball statistic comprising the number of bases a batter reaches from hits, with a single counting as one and a home run four. The **most total bases in an MLB game** is 19, by the LA Dodgers' Shawn Green in 2002. Green smashed four home runs, a single and a double against the Milwaukee Brewers.

2 NOVEMBER

In 2003, Margaret Okayo (KEN) completed the **fastest women's New York Marathon**, running 26 mi (42 km) through the streets of the Big Apple in 2 hr 22 min 31 sec. Her record has stood for more than 20 years. Okayo won four Marathon Majors in total, adding titles in London and Boston to her two triumphs in New York.

3 NOVEMBER

During a Ranji Trophy cricket match between Himachal Pradesh and Jammu & Kashmir in Chamba in 1999, Rajeev Nayyar (IND) was finally dismissed after a marathon knock of 271 that had spanned three days of play. Nayyar faced 728 balls and batted for a total of 16 hr 55 min –the **longest individual men's first-class cricket innings**. He remains the only player to have batted for more than 1,000 min. The match was drawn.

4 NOVEMBER

The Minnesota Vikings' Adrian Peterson (USA) exploded for the **most rushing yards in an NFL game** – 296 – against the San Diego Chargers in 2007. Having made just 43 rushing yards in the first two quarters, the rookie running back went for 253 yards in the second half, scoring three touchdowns.

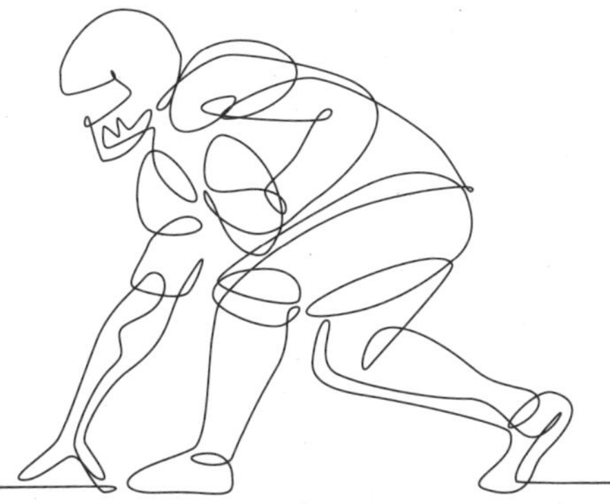

5 NOVEMBER

At the Women's Rugby World Cup in 2022, England defeated Canada 26–19 to advance to the final. The Red Roses had gone undefeated for three years, amassing the **most consecutive wins in international rugby union** – 30. They surpassed the previous all-time record of 24, held by Cyprus's men's team. But England's winning streak ended in dramatic fashion in the World Cup final, when they lost 34–31 to New Zealand having played much of the game with 14 players.

6 NOVEMBER

In 2017, skydiver Amber Forte (NOR, b. UK) achieved the **fastest women's parachuting speed (FAI-approved)**, clocking 283.7 km/h (176.2 mph) at the FAI World Cup of Wingsuit Flying in Overton, Nevada, USA. Wingsuits have fabric under the arms and between the legs to increase surface area. Forte has designs on becoming the first person to wingsuit across the English Channel.

7 NOVEMBER

In 2021, extreme sports star Eileen Gu (aka Gu Ailing, CHN, b. USA) became the **first woman to land a freeskiing double cork 1440**. The 18-year-old performed the acrobatic trick – comprising four full rotations with two flips while in midair – during a training session at the Austrian resort of Stubai.

8 NOVEMBER

Sri Lankan spinner Rangana Herath took his 433rd and final Test match wicket – that of England's Jos Buttler – during the first Test in Galle in 2018. Herath called time on his Test career having taken the **most Test wickets by a left-arm bowler**.

Leading Test lefties

PLAYER	COUNTRY	WICKETS	YEARS
Rangana Herath	Sri Lanka	433	1999–2018
Wasim Akram	Pakistan	414	1985–2002
Mitchell Starc	Australia	382	2011–
Daniel Vettori	New Zealand	362	1997–2014
Chaminda Vaas	Sri Lanka	355	1994–2009

9 NOVEMBER

In 1989, Dale Ellis (USA) of the Seattle SuperSonics logged the **most minutes in an NBA game**. He remained on court for 69 out of a possible 73 min during Seattle's quintuple-overtime 154–155 loss to the Milwaukee Bucks in Wisconsin. Ellis's teammate Xavier McDaniel played 68 min, taking second place on the all-time list. The marathon encounter remains the only NBA game to go into a fifth period of overtime in the shot-clock era.

> *"It was a fun game to play in. It reminded me of college basketball, because every possession in overtime was huge."*
>
> (Dale Ellis)

10 NOVEMBER

At the season-ending 2013 Valencian Grand Prix, Marc Márquez (ESP, b. 17 Feb 1993) became the **youngest MotoGP world champion** at 20 years 266 days old. In his debut season in the championship, the Honda rider won six out of 18 races to take the crown ahead of Jorge Lorenzo by four points.

11 NOVEMBER

In 2024, Matthieu Bonne (BEL) completed the **farthest men's six-day ultrarun** at an event in Balatonfüred, Hungary, covering 1,045.519 km (649.655 mi). That's around the same distance as between Paris and Madrid. Bonne beat the 19-year-old record of Yiannis Kouros by almost 9 km (5 mi).

> **The roots of the six-day ultrarun lie in the invention of competitive walking, or "pedestrianism", in 18th-century England. Six days was a popular timeframe as it allowed competitors to keep Sunday free for religious observance. In 1773, Foster Powell completed perhaps the first six-day race – against the clock – walking from London to York and back again in five days 18 hr 10 min.**

12 NOVEMBER

In 1942, Armand "Bep" Guidolin (CAN, b. 9 Dec 1925) of the Boston Bruins took to the ice aged 16 years 338 days. The **youngest NHL player**, his rise had been accelerated by the drain of players to military service during World War II. The Bruins lost 3–1 to the Toronto Maple Leafs; Guidolin went on to play 519 NHL games for three different teams, scoring 107 goals and providing 171 assists.

13 NOVEMBER

Filipino boxer Manny Pacquiao defeated Antonio Margarito in 2010 to win the WBC super welterweight belt – the eighth different weight at which he had become a world champion. "PacMan" had previously won titles at flyweight, super bantamweight, featherweight, super featherweight, lightweight, light welterweight and welterweight. This is the **most boxing world titles won in different weight divisions**.

14 NOVEMBER

At UFC 193 in 2015, Holly Holm (USA) achieved one of MMA's greatest upsets when she knocked out women's bantamweight champion Ronda Rousey in Melbourne, Australia. Holm, a former pro boxer who had claimed the inaugural WBA welterweight title in 2006, became the **first athlete to win a boxing and an MMA world title**.

15 NOVEMBER

Indian batsman Sachin Tendulkar was dismissed for 74 against the West Indies in his final Test innings in 2013. The "Little Master" retired having scored the **most runs in international cricket** – 34,357. His total comprised 18,426 runs in One-Day Internationals, 15,921 runs in Tests and 10 runs in his one and only T20 International. Tendulkar hit exactly 100 centuries and 164 fifties.

"Sachin Tendulkar is, in my time, the best player without doubt – daylight second."

(Shane Warne)

"Don't bowl [Tendulkar] bad balls. He hits the good ones for fours."

(Michael Kasprowicz)

"I have seen God. He bats at No.4 for India."

(Matthew Hayden)

16 NOVEMBER

In 2013, Lee Sang-hwa (KOR) completed the **fastest women's 500 m speed skating** – 36.36 sec – at the Utah Olympic Oval in Salt Lake City, USA. It was the third time she had broken the world record in eight days. Lee won two Olympic gold medals over the same distance, in 2010 and 2014.

17 NOVEMBER

In 2024, Norwegian goal-machine Erling Haaland (b. UK) hit a hat-trick against Kazakhstan to increase his record for the **most UEFA Nations League goals** to 19 in 16 games. The previous month, Haaland had scored twice against Slovenia to overtake Jørgen Juve's total of 33 international goals and become Norway's all-time leading scorer – at the age of just 24.

UEFA Nations League top scorers

PLAYER	COUNTRY	GOALS
Erling Haaland	Norway	19
Aleksandar Mitrović	Serbia	15
Cristiano Ronaldo	Portugal	12
Viktor Gyökeres	Sweden	10
Romelu Lukaku	Belgium	10
Vedat Muriqi	Kosovo	10

18 NOVEMBER

Zolani Tete (ZAF) recorded the **fastest knockout in a championship boxing fight** in 2017, winning his WBO bantamweight title bout with Siboniso Gonya after just 11 sec at the SSE Arena in Belfast, Northern Ireland. Tete caught his opponent with his first punch, a right hook, after 6 sec. With Gonya out cold, the referee ended the fight without finishing his 10 count.

19 NOVEMBER

In 2004, an NBA game between the Indiana Pacers and the Detroit Pistons descended into anarchy when a dispute over a foul escalated into a mass brawl that saw Pacers players exchanging blows with fans in the stands. The incident, dubbed the "Malice at the Palace", saw the Pacers' Ron Artest banned for 86 days – the **longest NBA suspension for an on-court incident**.

> *"I was lying down when I got hit with a liquid [from the crowd] – ice and glass on my chest and on my face. After that, it was self-defence."*
>
> (Ron Artest)

20 NOVEMBER

In 2021, Ryo Kiyuna (JPN) claimed the outright record for the **most wins of the World Karate Championships men's *kata***, winning his fourth title. Deriving from the early teachings of martial arts, *kata* is the choreographed display of karate moves and techniques. Practitioners are judged on their precision and athleticism.

21 NOVEMBER

Iran's Mehdi Taremi hit the **latest regular-time goal at the FIFA World Cup** at the 2022 tournament in Qatar. He converted a penalty after 12 min 30 sec of injury time had been added against England. It was only a consolation, however, as England won the group-stage game 6–2.

The **fastest goal at the FIFA World Cup** was scored in 2002 by Hakan Şükür for Türkiye, during their third-place play-off against South Korea. The "Bull of the Bosphorus" struck just 10.8 sec after kick-off. Türkiye ran out 3–2 winners.

22 NOVEMBER

In 1986, Mike Tyson (USA, b. 30 Jun 1966) became the **youngest world heavyweight boxing champion**, delivering a second-round knockout to Trevor Berbick for the WBC title at the age of 20 years 145 days. "Iron Mike" had already earned a fearsome reputation in the ring, winning all 27 of his previous pro bouts, 25 by KO.

23 NOVEMBER

Ed Reed (USA) of the Baltimore Ravens completed the **longest NFL interception return for a touchdown** in 2008. The safety picked off a pass from Philadelphia Eagles' quarterback Kevin Kolb in the Ravens' endzone and ran 107 yards to score. Reed beat the previous record of 106 yards, which had been set by... Ed Reed, back in 2004.

24 NOVEMBER

In the semi-final of the 2017 Rugby League World Cup, winger Valentine Holmes (AUS) scored six tries as Australia romped to a 54–6 victory over Fiji at the Suncorp Stadium in Brisbane, Queensland. Holmes recorded the **most tries in a Rugby League World Cup game** only a week after touching down five times against Samoa in the quarter-final.

25 NOVEMBER

In 2017, Irish runner Paul Robinson completed the **fastest Antarctic mile run** in 4 min 17.9 sec. The straight point-to-point course across the remote Union Glacier was measured four times by a GPS satellite to ensure that the distance was accurate. Accounting for wind chill, the temperature was -25°C (-13°F).

26 NOVEMBER

In 1989, the first Vendée Globe Challenge got underway in the French port of Les Sables-d'Olonne, with 13 seafarers setting out in 60-ft monohulls to sail around the world. The race was won by Titouan Lamazou, who returned to Sables on 15 Mar 1990. Known as the "Everest of the Seas", the Vendée Globe Challenge is the world's **longest non-stop solo sailing race**, spanning some 45,000 km (24,000 nautical mi). There have been 10 editions to date.

> “*It's like an unknown planet, a world apart where you experience a thousand crazy emotions.*
>
> (Sailor Clarisse Crémer on racing the Vendée Globe)”

27 NOVEMBER

At the 1956 Summer Olympics in Melbourne, Australia, Al Oerter (USA) secured his first discus gold medal with a first-round throw of 56.36 m (184 ft 10 in). The following year, he was nearly killed in an automobile accident. Oerter recovered, however, to defend his Olympic crown in 1960 and went on to win two more golds in 1964 and 1968 – the **most Olympic men's discus titles** (4).

28 NOVEMBER

In 1929, the NFL's Chicago Cardinals overcame their city rivals the Chicago Bears 40–6. All of the Cardinals' points were scored by full-back Ernie Nevers (USA), who rushed for six touchdowns and kicked four extra points. Almost 100 years later, this is still the **most individual points in an NFL game**.

Nicknamed "Big Dog", Ernie Nevers was an extraordinary sporting talent. His skills at running, kicking and passing made him one of American football's great "triple-threat men". His six rushing TDs against the Bears was matched by Alvin Kamara in 2020, but has never been surpassed. Nevers also played pro baseball, pitching three seasons in the American League for the St Louis Browns.

29 NOVEMBER

In 2014, Noriaki Kasai (JPN, b. 6 Jun 1972) became the **oldest winner of an FIS Ski Jumping World Cup event**, sharing first place with Simon Ammann in Ruka, Finland, at the age of 42 years 176 days. Kasai was still competing at the World Cup a full decade later, having entered more than 570 events.

30 NOVEMBER

The 2022 Mosconi Cup was the 29th edition of the annual nine-ball pool tournament contested by teams from the USA and Europe. The USA's roster included Earl "The Pearl" Strickland (USA, b. 8 Jun 1961), who at 61 years 175 days became the **oldest Mosconi Cup player**. It was the hot-tempered cueman's 15th appearance in the event.

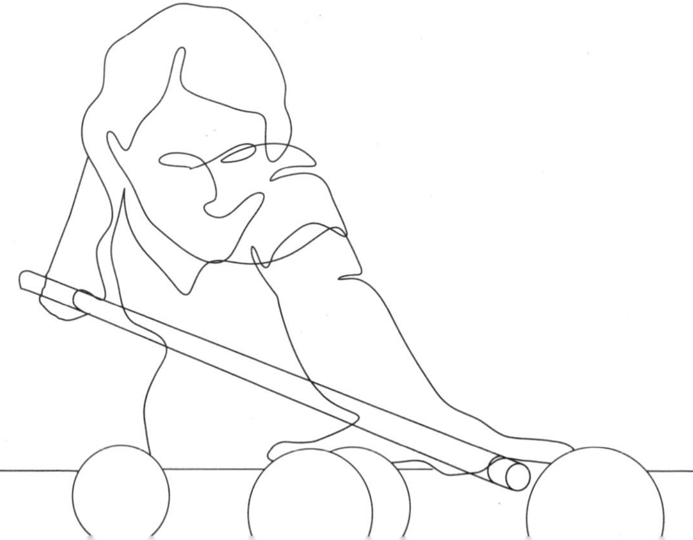

1 DECEMBER

In 2022, the England men's cricket team plundered 506 runs in just 75 overs on the opening day of the first Test against hosts Pakistan in Rawalpindi. This is the **most runs scored by a team on the first day of a Test match**. England reaped the rewards of their aggressively positive approach to Test cricket, which was dubbed "Bazball" after their coach, New Zealand's Brendon McCullum.

2 DECEMBER

The Memphis Grizzlies mauled the Oklahoma City Thunder 152–79 in 2021 to record the **greatest winning margin in an NBA game**. The 73-point blowout beat a record that had stood since 1991, when the Cleveland Cavaliers beat the Miami Heat by 68 points (148–80).

> *"It feels great to be in the history books, especially in front of our home crowd. And we did it one through 15. Everybody contributed, everybody played hard."*
>
> (Grizzlies guard De'Anthony Melton)

3 DECEMBER

The **first winner of the Women's Ballon d'Or** was crowned in 2018 – Norway's Ada Hegerberg. The Lyon striker had finished as top scorer in the 2017/18 Women's Champions League with 15 goals, including one in the final as the French powerhouses defeated Wolfsburg 4–1 to claim the third of their five consecutive European titles.

4 DECEMBER

On the opening day of pool's Mosconi Cup in 2017, Europe's Joshua Filler (DEU, b. 2 Oct 1997) defeated Dennis Hatch of the USA 5–4. Aged 20 years 63 days, Filler was the **youngest Mosconi Cup player**, beating the previous record of snooker legend Ronnie O'Sullivan, who played in 1996. Filler went on to earn the MVP award for the 2017 tournament, a feat he repeated in 2022 and 2023.

5 DECEMBER

Pole vaulter Armand Duplantis (SWE, b. USA, 10 Nov 1999) became the **youngest World Athlete of the Year** in 2020, winning the men's category aged 21 years 25 days. The man known as "Mondo" won all 16 competitions he entered that year, breaking the world record twice and raising the bar to 6.18 m (20 ft 3 in). To date, Duplantis has set 11 consecutive world records in the event.

On 4 Sep 2024, Duplantis faced off against 400 m hurdles world record holder Karsten Warholm in a 100 m exhibition race in Zurich. It was the pole vaulter who triumphed, in a time of 10.37 sec. As a forfeit, Warholm – a Norwegian – had to compete in a Sweden jersey.

6 DECEMBER

At the 2020 Sakhir Grand Prix in Bahrain, Racing Point's Sergio Pérez (MEX) claimed a dramatic victory after a first-lap crash left him at the back of the field. Pérez took the chequered flag for the first time in F1 on his 190th start – the **most races before a Formula One win**.

F1's longest waits for a win

DRIVER	TEAM	F1 DEBUT	FIRST WIN	RACE NO.
Sergio Pérez (MEX)	Racing Point	2011	2020 Sakhir	190
Carlos Sainz Jr (ESP)	Ferrari	2015	2022 British	150
Mark Webber (AUS)	Williams	2002	2009 German	130
Rubens Barrichello (BRA)	Ferrari	1993	2000 German	124
Jarno Trulli (ITA)	Renault	1997	2004 Monaco	117

7 DECEMBER

At the 2021 Scottish Open in Llandudno, Wales, Jimmy Robertson (UK) racked up the **highest score in a frame of professional snooker**. During his first-round match with Lee Walker, Robertson accrued 44 points in fouls and potted a single red before a clearance of 133 took his score to 178 – a full 31 points more than that on offer for a 147 maximum break.

8 DECEMBER

During a 2001 One-Day International at the Sinhalese Sports Club Ground in Colombo, Zimbabwe were skittled by home side Sri Lanka for just 38 runs. Pace bowler Chaminda Vaas took the **most wickets in a men's One-Day International** – eight, for a miserly 19 runs. His haul included a hat-trick. Sri Lanka needed just 4.2 overs to score the winning runs, wrapping up the entire game in just over two hours.

9 DECEMBER

In 2022, the so-called "Battle of Lusail" between Argentina and the Netherlands saw referee Antonio Mateu Lahoz (ESP) issue the **most yellow cards in a FIFA World Cup match** – 18. Following an ill-tempered 2–2 draw, Argentina won the penalty shootout 4–3. Ten of their players were booked, while the Dutch received eight yellows – including two for Denzel Dumfries, who was sent off after receiving his second caution during a post-shootout fracas.

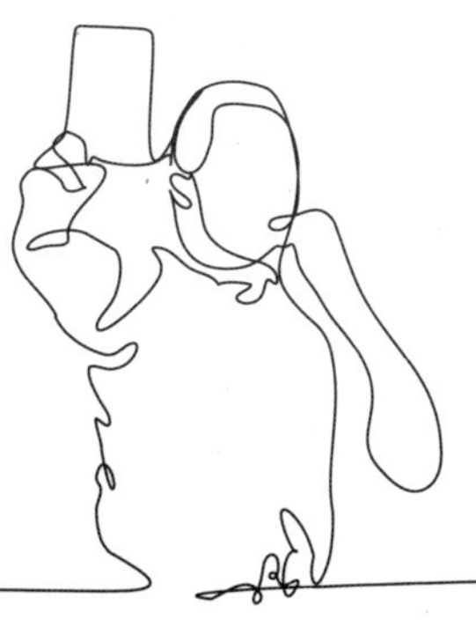

10 DECEMBER

At UFC 282 in 2022, high-school senior Raúl Rosas Jr (MEX, b. 8 Oct 2004) submitted Jay Perrin with a face crank to become the **youngest UFC fight winner** at 18 years 63 days old. Rosas Jr – nicknamed "El Niño Problema" – had already recorded six MMA victories before making his debut inside the Octagon.

11 DECEMBER

At the 2022 Honolulu Marathon in Hawaii, USA, Mathea Allansmith (USA, b. 31 May 1930) crossed the line aged 92 years 194 days to become the **oldest woman to complete a marathon**. A retired ophthalmologist who took up running in her mid-40s, Allansmith finished the course in 11 hr 19 min 49 sec.

"No matter what, I've got my running shoes on and I'm out the door six days per week."

(Mathea Allansmith)

12 DECEMBER

In the final of the 2017 Bangladesh Premier League, Chris Gayle (JAM) blasted 146 not out from 69 balls for the Rangpur Riders against the Dhaka Dynamites. His match-winning knock contained the **most sixes in a men's T20 innings** – 18. Gayle beat his own record by one.

Self-styled "Universe Boss" Chris Gayle is the only player to have hit the first ball of a Test match for six. He cleared the ropes off the opening delivery of Bangladesh off-spinner Sohag Gazi – who was making his Test debut – on 13 Nov 2012.

13 DECEMBER

In 1983, the Detroit Pistons and Denver Nuggets made history when they combined for the **most points in an NBA game**, 370, with the Pistons winning 186–184 after triple-overtime. The Nuggets' Kiki VanDeWeghe led all scorers with 51 points. There were 117 free throw attempts, but – despite the blizzard of points – each team hit only a single three-pointer.

14 DECEMBER

A First Division match between Arsenal and Aston Villa in 1935 ended with the Gunners inflicting a 7–1 defeat on their hosts. Striker Ted Drake (UK) scored all seven – the **most goals in an English top-flight football match**. Drake claimed he should have had an eighth, from a shot which bounced down off the crossbar but was ruled not have crossed the line. The record for a player in the English Premier League (est. 1992) is five goals, and has been achieved five times.

Five-goal EPL hauls

PLAYER	GAME	SCORE	DATE
Andy Cole (UK)	MANCHESTER UNITED vs Ipswich Town	9–0	4 Mar 1995
Alan Shearer (UK)	NEWCASTLE UNITED vs Sheffield Wednesday	8–0	19 Sep 1999
Jermain Defoe (UK)	TOTTENHAM HOTSPUR vs Wigan Athletic	9–1	22 Nov 2009
Dimitar Berbatov (BGR)	MANCHESTER UNITED vs Blackburn Rovers	7–1	27 Nov 2010
Sergio Agüero (ARG)	MANCHESTER CITY vs Newcastle United	6–1	3 Oct 2015

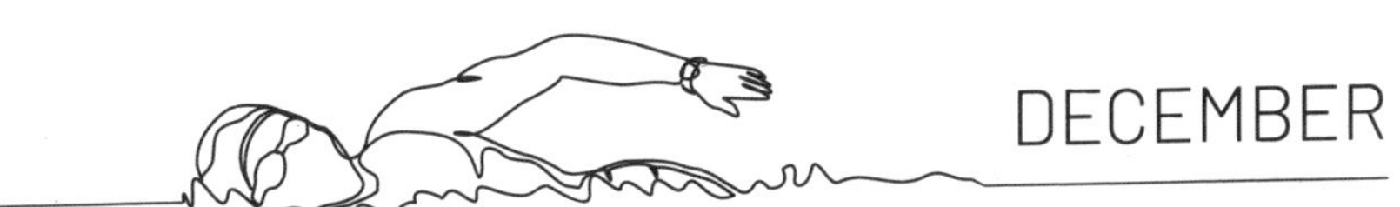

15 DECEMBER

At the 2024 World Aquatics Swimming Championships (25 m), Gretchen Walsh (USA) completed the **fastest short course women's 50 m freestyle**, completing two laps of the 25-m-long pool in 22.83 sec. Walsh set an astonishing 11 world records at the event in Budapest, Hungary – the most ever by a swimmer at a single championship.

16 DECEMBER

The Florida Panthers and the Washington Capitals played out the **longest NHL shootout** in 2014, matching one another for 19 rounds until the Panthers' Nick Bjugstad finally sealed the 2–1 win at the bottom of the 20th. Florida goaltender Roberto Luongo made a record 15 saves during the drama-filled duel, which lasted for almost 18 min at the BB&T Center in Sunrise, Florida, USA.

17 DECEMBER

During the first Test between New Zealand and Sri Lanka in 2018 at Wellington's Basin Reserve, the Black Caps closed their first innings on 578 with opener Tom Latham not out on 264. This is the **highest Test score by a cricketer carrying their bat**.

To date, players have carried their bat 57 times in men's Test cricket. Two batters have achieved the feat on three occasions: the West Indies' Desmond Haynes and South Africa's Dean Elgar. The lowest score by a player to have carried his bat is 26 not out, by South Africa's Bernard Tancred against England in 1889 – the first time the feat had been achieved.

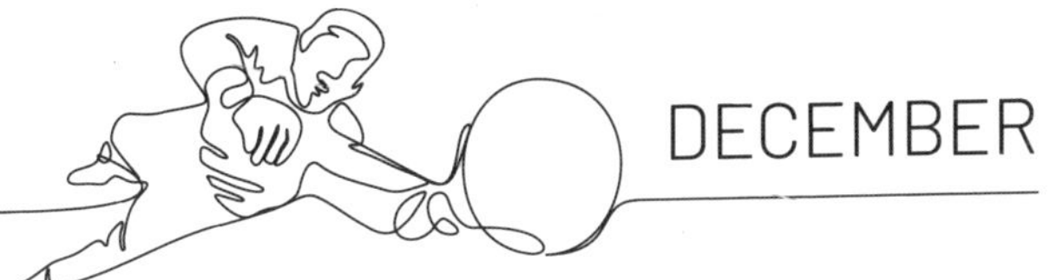

18 DECEMBER

In the final of the 2022 FIFA World Cup in Qatar, Argentina defeated France in a penalty shootout following a 3–3 draw after extra time. It was captain Lionel Messi's 26th World Cup game across five tournaments, overtaking Lothar Matthäus's record for the **most FIFA World Cup matches by a player**. Messi completed a fairytale tournament by scoring twice and converting Argentina's first penalty in the shootout.

Messi at the World Cup

YEAR	MATCHES	GOALS	ROUND
2006	3	1	Quarter-final
2010	5	0	Quarter-final
2014	7	4	Final
2018	4	1	Round of 16
2022	7	7	Winner

19 DECEMBER

Dublin collected their sixth Sam Maguire Cup in a row in 2020, defeating Mayo 2–14 to 0–15 at Croke Park. This is the **most consecutive wins of the All-Ireland Senior Football Championship**. Gaelic football's showpiece game has taken place every year bar one since 1887, and is traditionally held in September on the 35th Sunday of the year.

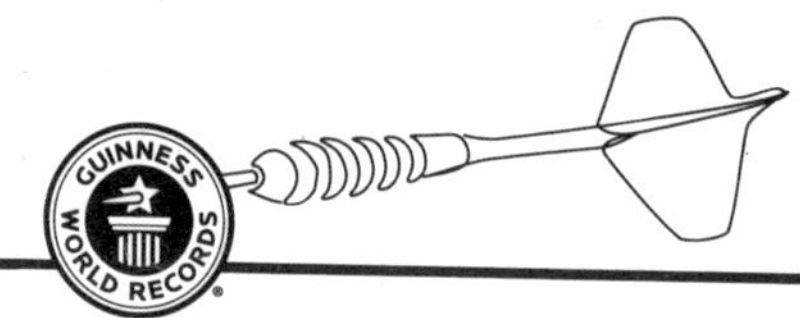

20 DECEMBER

In 2023, Luke Littler (UK, b. 21 Jan 2007) became the **youngest person to win a match at the PDC World Darts Championship**. The fresh-faced darter was aged 16 years 333 days when he downed Christian Kist 3–0 at London's Alexandra Palace. "Luke the Nuke" made it all the way to the world championship final, losing out 7–4 to Luke Humphries.

21 DECEMBER

In 1891, students from the International Young Men's Christian Association Training School in Springfield, Massachusetts, USA, played the **first basketball game**. They were arranged in two teams of nine and used peach baskets for hoops. The rules had been drawn up by Canadian PE teacher James Naismith.

22 DECEMBER

Boxer Khaosai Galaxy (THA, b. Sura Saenkham) defeated Armando Castro in 1991 to defend his WBA super flyweight title for the 19th time in a row. The hard-hitting southpaw, who had won the belt in 1984, retired soon afterwards, having won 47 of his 48 pro boxing bouts. He still holds the record for the **most consecutive super flyweight world title defences**.

23 DECEMBER

In 1978, ice hockey centre Bryan Trottier (CAN) scored three goals and laid on three assists during the second period of the New York Islanders' 9–4 victory against the New York Rangers. This is the **most points in an NHL regular-season period** – six. Trottier's mark was equalled on 17 Mar 2021 by Mika Zibanejad (SWE), who managed a hat-trick and three assists for the Rangers during the second period of a 9–0 win over the Philadelphia Flyers.

24 DECEMBER

Quarterback Eli Manning and wide receiver Victor Cruz of the New York Giants combined for a 99-yard touchdown against the New York Jets in 2011. This equalled the record for the **longest NFL pass completion** – the longest possible in the game involving a forward pass – which had been achieved on 12 previous occasions.

The first team to make a 99-yard passing play were the Washington Commanders (then Redskins), against the Pittsburgh Pirates on 15 Oct 1939. Washington repeated the feat in 1963 and 1968, and remain the only NFL side to do so more than once.

25 DECEMBER

In 2020, Iranian freestyler Arash Ahmadi Tifakani achieved the **longest distance juggling a football** – an astonishing 21.2 km (13.1 mi) in Minab, Iran. He kept the ball in the air for 212 reps of a 100-m course. Tifakani also holds the record for the **longest time balancing a football on the head**: 8 hr 42 min 12 sec.

26 DECEMBER

The **highest attendance for a single day of a Test cricket match** was set in 2013, on day one of the fourth Ashes Test between Australia and England. A total of 91,092 people packed out the Melbourne Cricket Ground in Victoria. They watched an England batting line-up traumatised by Aussie pace bowler Mitchell Johnson creep to 226 for 6 by stumps. England would go on to lose the series 5–0.

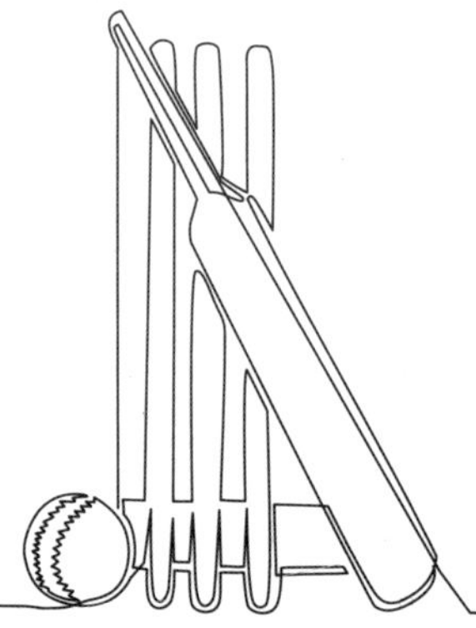

27 DECEMBER

The 2017 Sydney Hobart Yacht Race was won by *LDV Comanche* after the initial winner of "line honours", *Wild Oats XI*, was handed a 1-hr time penalty for its role in a near-collision at the start of the race. The winning time was 1 day 9 hr 15 min 24 sec – the **fastest completion of the Sydney Hobart Yacht Race**.

> First held in 1945, the Sydney Hobart Yacht Race gets underway on Boxing Day each year. Yachts race 628 nautical mi (1,163 km) from Sydney in New South Wales, Australia, to Hobart on the island of Tasmania. "Line honours" are awarded to the first yacht to cross the finish line.

28 DECEMBER

At the US Olympic Trials in 2013, Heather Bergsma (then Richardson) produced the **fastest women's speed skating 2 x 500 m**. She completed two 500-m skates in a combined time of 1 min 14.19 sec at the Utah Olympic Oval in Salt Lake City – a high-altitude track renowned for super-fast times.

29 DECEMBER

At UFC 232 in 2018, Amanda Nunes (BRA) brutally dismantled Cris Cyborg in less than a minute of their featherweight championship bout at The Forum in Inglewood, California, USA. Already the women's bantamweight title holder, Nunes became the **first female UFC fighter to hold two titles simultaneously**. Alone among the UFC's other double champions – Conor McGregor, Daniel Cormier and Henry Cejudo – Nunes went on to defend her titles while holding both of them.

30 DECEMBER

In 2011, endurance runner Pat Farmer (AUS) set out for the South Pole from Antarctica's Union Glacier Camp on the **longest polar ultramarathon**. He ran 50–70 km (30–45 mi) for up to 20 hr per day, arriving at his destination on 18 Jan 2012, having covered a distance of 1,198 km (744.4 mi). It was the final leg of Farmer's "Pole to Pole" challenge, which saw him run *c.* 21,000 km (13,050 mi) from the North Pole to the South.

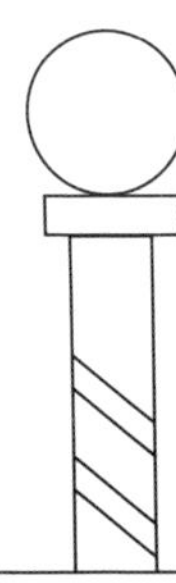

31 DECEMBER

In 2012, Chris Adam (CAN) reached the end of 366 days of perpetual putting during which he completed the **most holes of golf in a year** – 14,625. Chris played 809 full rounds and seven half-rounds at the King Kamehameha Golf Club on the Hawaiian island of Maui. He averaged 40 holes a day while also running his ice-cream parlour, playing on despite suffering from shoulder and wrist pain, broken toes and a strained back.